JOHARI WINDOW

	Known to self	Known to self
Known to others	**ARENA** *(My public self)*	**BLIND SPOT** *(My overlooked self)*
Not known to others	**FAÇADE** *(My secret self)*	**UNKNOWN** *(My unknown self)*

THE BASIC PILLARS IN DISC

Task-oriented
and issue-oriented

COMPLIANCE

DOMINANCE

How you react
to rules and
regulations

How you approach
problems and deal
with challenges

Waiting / Introvert

Action / Extrovert

How you react
to change

How you cooperate
with and try
to influence
other people

STABILITY

INFLUENCE

Person and
relationship-oriented

Surrounded
by Psychopaths

ALSO BY THOMAS ERIKSON
Surrounded by Idiots

. . . .

Surrounded by Psychopaths

How to Protect Yourself
from Being Manipulated
and Exploited
in Business (and in Life)

Thomas Erikson

ST. MARTIN'S
ESSENTIALS
New York

First published in the United States by St. Martin's Essentials, an imprint of St. Martin's Publishing Group

SURROUNDED BY PSYCHOPATHS. Copyright © 2017 by Thomas Erikson. Translation © 2020 by Rod Bradbury. All rights reserved. Printed in the United States of America. For information, address St. Martin's Publishing Group, 120 Broadway, New York, NY 10271.

www.stmartins.com

Library of Congress Cataloging-in-Publication Data

Names: Erikson, Thomas, 1965– author.
Title: Surrounded by psychopaths : how to protect yourself from being manipulated and exploited in business (and in life) / Thomas Erikson.
Other titles: Omgiven av psykopater. English
Description: First U.S. edition. | New York : St. Martin's Essentials, [2020] | "Originally published in Sweden by Forum in 2017"—Verso. | Includes bibliographical references and index.
Identifiers: LCCN 2020024221 | ISBN 9781250763884 (hardcover) | ISBN 9781250786036 (international, sold outside the U.S., subject to rights availability) | ISBN 9781250763891 (ebook)
Subjects: LCSH: Manipulative behavior. | Personality. | Psychopaths.
Classification: LCC BF632.5 .E7513 2020 | DDC 158.2—dc23
LC record available at https://lccn.loc.gov/2020024221

Our books may be purchased in bulk for promotional, educational, or business use. Please contact your local bookseller or the Macmillan Corporate and Premium Sales Department at 1-800-221-7945, extension 5442, or by email at MacmillanSpecialMarkets@macmillan.com.

Originally published in Sweden by Forum in 2017

First U.S. Edition: 2020

10 9 8 7 6 5 4 3 2 1

Contents

Loving you was like going to war; I never came back the same.

—WARSAN SHIRE

Surrounded
by Psychopaths

Introduction

> Our society is run by insane people for insane objectives.
>
> —John Lennon

Imagine that an extremely attractive person of the sex you prefer sits down opposite you and exclaims with a smile: "You are the most fantastic person I've ever met!" You immediately sense that this is for real, that the person is sincere. They ask questions and want to know everything about you. They don't talk about themselves, and they look at you as if you were the only person in the room. Their attention leaves you glowing, lit up in a way you've never felt before. This other person says the kinds of things you've waited a lifetime to hear. They somehow understand precisely who you are, the inner quirks of your personality, your every like and dislike. You feel as if you have finally found your soul mate. Through some magic, this person has gotten straight to your heart in a way you have never felt before.

Can you see it in your mind's eye? Can you imagine the feeling? It would be fantastic, right?

And now the question: Can you look yourself in a mirror and honestly say that this wouldn't affect you? That you aren't susceptible to the lure of romantic nonsense and that you would immediately become suspicious and realize that this person wants something completely different? If not your body, then probably your money.

Think a moment before you answer. Because if you've never been in such a situation, then you'll never see the danger. This person is going to tell you their secrets, and they are going to get you to reveal yours. You will answer all their probing questions, the sole purpose of which is to find out as much as possible about you.

A few years ago, I wrote a book called *Surrounded by Idiots*. The book was about the basics of the DISC language, one of the most powerful methods in the world to describe human communication and the differences in human behavior patterns. The book was a success, which I hadn't really expected. I believe part of the reason for its success is that a lot of people are, like me, fascinated by human behavior—the behavior of others and, above all, their own. And I might as well admit it: *ME, I'm an interesting person!* At least to myself.

The behavior categories I use, in that first book as well as in this one, are based on William Moulton Marston's theories and consist of four main types of people, each of which is associated with a color: Red for dominance, Yellow for influence, Green for stability, and Blue for compliance. The following chapters provide an overview of what the colors mean in practice. These categories are a tool that can help answer many (but not all) of our questions about how people function.

People are too complex to be described completely, but the more you understand, the easier it is to identify the outliers. This method of behavior categorization encompasses perhaps 80 percent of the entire puzzle. Quite a lot, but far from everything. There are always other elements that we need to take into consideration to understand someone's behavior: gender, age, cultural differences, motivation, intelligence, interests, experiences of every sort, birth order, and countless other factors. For the sake of simplicity, let's say that the puzzle has an awful lot of pieces.

Now for the Problem

As the book became more and more popular around the world, there were some people who chose to use the DISC system in a malicious way. This was never my intention. In this book, I want to make you aware of such individuals, of people who would try to manipulate you, and to give you the tools to protect yourself. I'm often asked if an individual can have *all* the colors—be a little bit Red, Yellow, Green, and Blue. "I'm a bit of each color," readers have written to me in emails. "Is that possible?" It can certainly feel possible. I act Red sometimes, Yellow and Green often, but on other occasions I am undoubtedly Blue. The reason why this is possible is actually quite simple: We all have the ability to use whichever type of behavior we want, thanks to the fact that we are intelligent beings who can think for ourselves. As their self-awareness increases, a Yellow person will learn that it's time to close their mouth and open their ears. And a Green person can learn to express their heartfelt opinion even if that might lead to conflict. But the bottom line is that normally two colors dominate a person's behavior.

An Unpleasant Experience

Approximately one year after *Surrounded by Idiots* was published, I had a strange encounter. A young man came up to me after a lecture I had given at a university. He stood right in front of me, face to face, more or less pushing aside others who also wanted to ask questions. With an intense gaze, he said that he didn't recognize himself in *any* of the colors. I asked him what he meant by that, and he said that none of the behaviors I had described fitted him. He thought he was a fifth color. He also wanted to know more about how to best interact with the other colors, but his choice of words was interesting: He told me he wanted to know "how to take advantage of this knowledge."

Okay.

I gave him a standard answer since I didn't have time to start analyzing him then and there, and when he realized that he wasn't going to get anywhere with his questions, he stepped aside. But he didn't leave; instead, he remained standing a few yards away, observing me the whole time until I packed up all my things.

"Observed" is not quite the right word. In fact, he stared at me in an almost embarrassing way for perhaps ten minutes. I saw people come up to him, say hello, and smile. And every time he smiled back. But he wasn't really smiling at all. He *pretended* to smile. His face was distorted into a weird, strange grimace, a sort of imitation of a smile. Some of the people he smiled at noticed and reacted with a questioning look, while others didn't seem to think there was anything out of the ordinary. And after every "smile," he went back to his serious, concentrated staring. At me. It was decidedly uncomfortable.

And what did he mean by "take advantage" of the DISC system?

It struck me that the young man was right about one thing: the DISC language doesn't apply to everybody. A part of the population can't be categorized. We should be very careful of such unpleasant, maybe even dangerous, types of people. We've all heard the stories of the master manipulators, the con men, the imposters. *How could he trick me so totally?* their victims wonder. *Why didn't I see that he was a con man?*

The reason? Because these individuals know how they can use your own behavior against you. They have an instinctive understanding of how to manipulate a person to do virtually anything. And they can con virtually anybody using what *they learn about them.* Their purpose is always the same: to get what they want. They leave behind a trail of chaos and disorder.

The question is this: If a person doesn't have a personality of their own, but simply mirrors whomever is in front of them, who is that person? They are not Red or Yellow, and definitely not Green or Blue. Are they all the colors? A fifth color? The answer is none of these. They are something much worse, something that cannot be categorized in the way we categorize normal people. They are people who don't have a personality of their own; instead, they mimic whatever they see for their own gain. They are a type of chameleon with a hidden agenda that only they know of. And we can be certain that this agenda only ever benefits them.

Instead of identifying these people as a fifth color or a combination of all the colors, I define them as having no color at all. Because a person who doesn't really have a genuine personality, who is always at least partially acting, is not a real person. They are more a shadow, a reflection of reality but not properly real. They are a sort of walking fraud on two legs. If you have met this type of individual, you'll know what I'm talking about.

But who *are* they, these people? What sort of people try to mimic what other people do? And what can their goal be?

Pretending to Be Like Everybody Else

To put it plainly: they are predators in human form. Does that sound dramatic? The reason for that is very simple: it *is* dramatic! These individuals end up harming most people they come into contact with, and often the victims don't even know who is responsible for the disarray.

That, dear reader, is what psychopaths do.

Luckily, they're all locked up in jail. Right?

Psychopaths are living in society just like the rest of us. They infiltrate companies and organizations, where they get comparatively little work done and only in exceptional cases do they make any positive contributions. They rarely offer to get the bill at the restaurant, and they never have any money when household expenses have to be paid. They are often unfaithful, manipulative, and duplicitous. They are notorious liars; most of them lie when there isn't even any reason to do so. They can fool anyone into believing them, and they turn everything you say against you. But they are often extremely popular. A lot of people like them, place them on a pedestal, and even respect them.

How is this possible? you might well ask yourself. Good question. How could we like a person who is so duplicitous? *Not me,* you're thinking to yourself, *I would hate them from the very start.* Exactly. If you knew their real self, you would hate them. But you wouldn't know. Because they wouldn't allow it to show. With a bit of luck, you might eventually discover it. In the best case, you'd realize who they were before things are desperate, when you've lost your job, and you are cut off from all the people you once called your friends.

But hang on a moment, you might be thinking. *Psychopaths are serial murderers and violent criminals. Most of these maniacs are obviously in prison.*

If only that was the case! It is true that a lot of them are behind bars since they have not been able to control their impulses. They are violent and sometimes crazy, to put it plainly. When they see something they want, they simply take it, often with violence, which quickly gives them away. But the majority of all psychopaths are not behind bars. The more intelligent psychopaths and those who don't commit serious violent crimes are walking around among us just like everybody else. They are people who will stop at nothing to get what they want. And you have certainly come across some of them.

But are we really surrounded by them?

The title *Surrounded by Psychopaths* was chosen with care, since there are far more psychopaths than I think most people are aware of. I want to show you how to recognize a master manipulator and to protect yourself, should you come across one.

What Are the Consequences?

The strange behavior of the young man at the lecture troubled me for several months. Those staring eyes, the artificial smile. It was all so weird. What happened to him? I got the answer on a subsequent trip when I returned to the university. I sought out the chair of the department where I had lectured and asked about the young man. Who was he? Did the department head know anything about him? The answer I got was horrific.

The young man was an employee who had been caught embezzling almost one hundred thousand dollars from the university before he was reported to the police by the department head. But by then he had gotten two women in the department pregnant. He managed to get one of them dismissed for sexual harassment (against him!), and the other woman tried to commit suicide after the affair was revealed (she had been married many years). Two postgraduate members of staff were on sick leave with chronic fatigue syndrome, after the young man had spread gossip and created chaos among the staff. The head of the department had resigned, and everything was in turmoil. Nobody knew what they should do, their research had been forgotten, and the department was falling apart.

But the young man had learned to smile. He had learned how to give the impression of being a nice, likable guy. He got away with it for two years before he was kicked out. Nobody suspected him.

He had an explanation for everything. And it was always somebody else's fault.

With a trembling voice, the department head told me that the young man had been let free after convincing the police as well as the prosecutor that he had embezzled the money *at the suggestion of the department head*. And the department head—with thirty-eight years at the university—had almost been prosecuted himself. Of course, the money was gone, and the evidence was so vague that nothing could be done to convict the real swindler. I asked what had happened to the young man. The department head told me that he had just gotten a new job at an IT company. He was now in charge of a project involving a large investment and was going to lead the company to new heights.

And so I learned that the young man at my lecture had indeed learned "*how to take advantage of the DISC system.*"

When the department head had finished his story, tears were running down his cheeks. It was terrible to see.

If I'd had the chance, I would have analyzed this young man. What would the analysis show? To be honest, I don't know.

The most frightening thing is that he is still out there. And if you bump into him or someone like him, it's critical that you know how to react. Because if he can sniff out your weaknesses, he will press all the buttons he can to destroy you. Not because he hates you or because he has some personal motivation. But because that is what psychopaths do. They take what they want from you. Using any means whatsoever. The consequences don't matter.

They seduce and deceive. They lie and manipulate. They are thieves and parasites. And they get their energy from destroying other people. That is their primary fuel.

Exaggerated? Not at all. After you read this book, you might find it difficult to sleep at night. If that happens, I apologize in advance.

I am going to explain how to recognize a psychopath, how to recognize people with psychopathic traits, and most importantly I will show you what you can do about psychopaths.

Another Book About Psychopaths?

After *Surrounded by Idiots* was published, I gave lectures throughout Europe on the DISC system. The book put focus on certain things I had always taken for granted. People are different. Obviously. We already knew that. But how different, and in what way? And, above all, how do you deal with those differences?

The color-based DISC language that William Moulton Marston laid the foundations for explains quite a lot about how people function. But, as I mentioned earlier, it does not explain everything.

Marston was one of the first well-known psychologists who carried out research on healthy people. Both Jung and Freud primarily devoted themselves to the mentally ill. Can you fit everybody into the DISC system? No, actually you can't. It only works with neurotypical persons—the type of people Marston studied. If you have some sort of diagnosis such as borderline personality disorder, severe autism, schizophrenia, or the like—or psychopathy—it simply does not work.

How Many Psychopaths Are There Really?

But hold on there, you might say. *Psychopaths are so rare that they're hardly worth worrying about. They can't be more than 0.1 (or even 0.2 or 0.3) percent of the population.* I can understand why you would think that. But there are more psychopaths than you imagine. According to the latest scientific findings, they comprise between 2 and 4 percent of the population. That is a significant number of people. As a point of comparison, I devoted quite a lot of pages in my previous book to people that are completely Red in their behavior, and they only comprise about 0.5 percent of the population.

Just think about it: if you were a shepherd with one thousand sheep and you heard that there were two wolves in the vicinity, what would you want to know more about? The sheep . . . or the wolves? Of course you would want to keep track of the wolves. Even though there aren't that many, and even if they aren't going to kill all the sheep they come across, it's a good idea to understand how a wolf thinks and to know one when you see it. Because once it has decided to attack, it's already too late. Then it will take whatever it wants.

When it comes to psychopaths, we're concerned about not only their primary victims but also the effect they have on their surroundings. An enormous number of people are affected by psychopaths' behavior, because the impact is vast. The damage they cause has far-reaching consequences. They always drag many people down with them.

This book is about how you can protect yourself from this behavior. As my starting point, I will use Marston's system with the four colors to show how the strengths and weaknesses of different behavior types play into the hands of an evil-minded psychopath. They will turn your weaknesses against you. That is one of the reasons why therapy does not work for psychopaths. They cannot be healed.

If you haven't read *Surrounded by Idiots,* I will explain some of the science behind the four-color system in the coming pages so you will have a better grasp of the terminology in the book and the reasoning behind the examples. If you've already read my previous book and think you already know the system 100 percent, be patient. Remember repetition is the key to knowledge.

> The closer to the truth, the better the lie, and the truth itself, when it can be used, is the best lie.
>
> —Isaac Asimov

An Example of Psychopathy

My first example of everyday psychopathy is one I experienced my-self. I have written several novels in addition to nonfiction, and after my first thriller had been published a young woman who wanted to be a writer contacted me via email. She had read my book and thought it was fantastic and asked if I could help with her own writing. My interactions with readers are simple. I really do appreciate all the mes-sages from people who have read my books, and I encourage you to share your opinion of this book with me. I'd love to hear from you. But I don't normally respond with more than one message. I don't start long dialogues, for the simple reason that I don't wish to work 24/7. I responded to her with a sort of standard answer and didn't think any more about it. But this woman continued to email me again and again, her tone becoming more aggressive when I didn't reply.

Some time later, my then-partner received an email from the same young woman—now using another name—which claimed that she was in a relationship with me and that we were going to get married. Both my partner and I were flabbergasted. In addition, the email con-tained a long list of nasty accusations against me. For example, the young woman claimed that I had had relationships with almost one hundred women and had gotten at least twenty of them pregnant. All within a few months. (This eventually led to my reporting her to the police.) There was far more of this craziness, but I can't describe everything. In all, my partner received about fifty emails with vary-ing content, but all on the same theme.

While this was going on, I was also receiving deeply romantic emails from the same young woman. She missed me so very much. She longed to see me again. Shouldn't we go and have a look at that apartment in the center of Stockholm together? From my Facebook profile, which at the time was completely public, she had gathered a large amount of information about me and my private life, which meant that some of things she wrote sounded quite credible. (Be warned: you don't know who sees what you do on the internet or what they can use it for.)

This went on for about six months before the police managed to stop her. It was a case of severe stalking. With the help of social media, the woman managed to cause me a lot of problems, particularly with a large number of writer colleagues. For me, it was all very embarrassing and horrible—at first, I didn't even know who she was.

A mental case, you're thinking. *An ordinary maniac. There are lots of them out there.*

Could be. But the pattern was there. The police investigation revealed that the woman had done the same thing at least once before. In that case, too, the man was much older than she was and a writer. You've probably heard of him. He took it so hard that he retired from his job. I talked with him several times to try to understand what was happening, but neither of us could fathom what the woman was really trying to achieve, apart from some sort of wild revenge because I hadn't helped her fulfill her writing dreams.

In their book *Female Psychopaths,* Lisbet Duvringe and Mike Florette write, "Revenge tastes good and they [the psychopaths] delight in destroying; they enjoy it. Female psychopaths especially seem to delight in looking for emotional revenge, social aggression, and then wreak havoc in the form of rumors that create manipulative, uncertain and threatening relationships. It is a type of destructive revenge that is not as visible as physical violence and is thus harder to identify."

I know exactly what it feels like to be at the receiving end of that behavior. The police finally took the young woman in for questioning, and after that, all the harassment stopped as if by magic. Remarkable, isn't it? When she was questioned by the police, she tried to suggest that someone else had been responsible, which reinforced my belief that she wasn't mentally ill. If she had had a diagnosis, some sort of disorder or compulsion, then she wouldn't have been able to stop herself so suddenly. But the entire time, she was fully aware of what she was doing. Things started to get too hot for her, and she presumably moved on to new hunting grounds, where she could continue her perverted behavior.

The police said that they had never met such a believable liar before. The woman seemed to believe her own words. Despite the fact that the police could show concrete evidence that she was responsible for the harassment and stalking (they had gone through her computer and found all they needed), she denied everything. And it didn't stop at that. She went on the offensive, by accusing me of threatening her. Suddenly it was *me* who was harassing *her*. She accused me of threatening to kill her, of having hired professional hit men that I, for some bizarre reason, had contact with. Serious allegations, to put it mildly. The only thing that saved me from being linked with this person was that I could easily show that I had not been in the various places where she claimed we had met.

The *pattern* of psychopathic behavior was there. This psychopath aimed to destroy my life and my writing career. She sought revenge for my refusing to communicate with her about her own writing, I guess. This time it didn't succeed. But she did manage to destroy my relationship with my partner. Our relationship was so badly strained by the whole exhausting nightmare that we finally went our separate ways. By that time, my former partner had become so scared that she developed true paranoia. She sat for hours every day on social media, searching for the woman and waiting for her to post. Nothing I said could stop her.

The young woman in question continued her life. On Facebook, I

SURROUNDED BY PSYCHOPATHS

could see that she was joyfully entertaining herself with a man on a yacht. She didn't seem to suffer the slightest, while my partner had become pathologically jealous and isolated me from everything— even from my children—so that this wouldn't happen again. When I couldn't even say hello to the staff in the shoe shop or talk with the waitress when we had dinner out at a restaurant without being subject to a veritable cross-examination, I realized that everything was lost. And I had never even met the young woman in real life.

How many people were affected?

How many people did this psychopath succeed in hurting? Let's count. Me. Both my children. My partner. Her three children. My father and my poor mother. My sister and all of her family. My co-workers in the company where I worked while all of this was going on. All the people that I counted as my friends.

One psychopath—perhaps fifty victims. One of fifty. Two percent of the population. There we have it again.

I didn't tell this story to get your sympathy. I have put the incident behind me. But I want to show that anybody can be affected. None of us is immune to this type of behavior, and—obviously—I am now much more cautious of people I meet. Hopefully it isn't too noticeable, but I know that there are between two to four psychopaths for every hundred people. So nowadays I pay more attention to weird behavior.

But however unpleasant that situation was for me and my friends and family, it is nothing compared with what happens in more extreme situations, because psychopaths can reach very far in their quest for power.

Some societies have developed mechanisms for isolating psychopaths— take, for example, the Inuits. Sometimes, when the men had to go out on long hunting expeditions, someone said he felt sick or pretended that he was wounded. Since he couldn't go along with the rest of the men, he stayed back at the village. When the hunters came back three months later, the village had burnt down and all the women were pregnant.

So what did the Inuits do with the guilty man? They put him on an ice floe.

A Far Worse Example

If I say "Adolf Hitler," what comes to mind?

Hitler set the world on fire, and this eventually cost the lives of about sixty million people, in addition to all the rest of the suffering that affected hundreds of millions of people throughout the world. The material costs of the Second World War are presumably impossible to estimate. What if all these innumerable billions had been used for something good instead?

If I claim that Hitler was an out-and-out psychopath, would you protest? Probably not. Pure instinct makes us feel in our very bones that he must have been a maniac. And you'll certainly have wondered: Why didn't anybody see what a lunatic he was? Why wasn't he stopped in time? How could all of Germany allow him to do what he did? Why didn't anybody put a stop to it?

Good questions, all of them. And the answer is that psychopaths are clever at fooling those around them.

But from a purely scientific perspective, how do we *know* that Hitler was a psychopath? Kevin Dutton, the author of the book *The Good Psychopath's Guide to Success,* used a personality test to diagnose psychopathy in adults. The test is called PPI-R (Psychopathic Personality Inventory–Revised), and it was originally developed by Scott Lilienfeld and Brian Andrews to evaluate certain character traits in noncriminal populations.

The intention was to comprehensively list psychopathic traits without paying special attention to antisocial or criminal behavior.

The test also contains methods to discover deviations within leadership or generally irresponsible responses.

The PPI-R test reveals eight specific factors:

- Machiavellian Egocentricity—a lack of empathy and sense of detachment from others for the sake of achieving one's own goals
- Social Influence—the ability to charm and fool others
- Cold-heartedness—a distinct lack of emotion, guilt, or regard for others' feelings
- Carefree Disorganization—difficulty in planning ahead and considering the consequences of one's actions
- Fearlessness—an eagerness for risk-seeking behaviors, as well as a lack of the fear that normally goes with them
- Blame Externalization—inability to take responsibility for one's actions, instead blaming others or rationalizing one's own deviant behavior
- Rebellious Nonconformity—a disregard for social norms and socially acceptable behaviors
- Stress Immunity—a lack of typical reactions to traumatic or otherwise stress-inducing events

Scientists have divided these factors into subcategories and grouped them to create a useful model. The two categories are Fearless Dominance and Self-Centered Impulsivity. After studying the comprehensive historical material that is available on Hitler, Dutton could place Hitler high on the list of individuals with severe psychopathic traits. This isn't really especially surprising, is it? Hitler, however, did not come as high as Saddam Hussein or Idi Amin. Or, for that matter, King Henry VIII of England. You can read the entire study, "What Psychopaths and Politicians Have in Common," in the September–October issue of *American Scientific Mind,* published in 2016.

So It's Only Dictators and Tyrants?

However, it gets really interesting when Dutton uses the same tool to examine other well-known leaders from history, looking at how they made decisions while being fully aware of how these decisions would affect other people. Almost as high on the list as Hitler, Dutton finds, strange though it may seem, is the man's nemesis: Winston Churchill.

And while we are on the subject of American presidents (and that particular role does of course have a considerable influence on the rest of the world), there is even a list of which presidents exhibit most psychopathic traits. Dutton interviewed people who consider themselves experts on particular presidents—for example, historians and academic researchers, as well as a number of individuals who have actually worked with former presidents. Without going too deep into the technicalities, below I list how the respective presidents "score" within the two subcategories: Fearless Dominance and Self-Centered Impulsivity.

The Winners Are . . . the Most Charming Imps

Right at the top of Dutton's list we find John F. Kennedy. Number two is Bill Clinton. Both of these men made a name for themselves as sympathetic, empathetic, and winning personalities—skillful orators who are clever at winning people's confidence. Nice guys, strictly speaking, but they did have quite a bit going on on the side. Documented promiscuity, to name only one activity. A couple of notches lower down, we find Theodore Roosevelt, George W. Bush, Richard Nixon, and Lyndon B. Johnson. Examples of presidents who totally lack psychopathic traits are Jimmy Carter, George Washington, Abraham Lincoln, Harry S. Truman, and, in fact, most of the others.

It might seem strange that popular and successful presidents can rank so highly in such a serious study, but after you've read this book, you will understand how they ended up there.

Why Should You Read *Surrounded by Psychopaths*?

My purpose with this book is not to frighten you or make you suspicious of other people—on the contrary. What I want is for you to learn which people you can trust and which are perhaps driven by some hidden agenda. Regardless of whether you are a CEO who is looking for a new manager, a romantic who feels that you have finally met the One, or an adult who still doesn't understand why you feel ill every time you meet your mother, with the help of this book you'll be able to recognize who is genuine and who is not. A smart, informed approach to each of your relationships is preferable to one that leads to catastrophe for: the relationship, your emotions and self-confidence, and your finances. Many a person who has been the victim of a psychopath loses the will to go on living. They give up and lose their joy in life.

So let's take a look at what this is all about!

1

What Actually Is a Psychopath?

I never encourage deceit and falsehood, especially if you have got a bad memory, it's the worst enemy a fellow can have. The fact is, truth is your truest friend, no matter what the circumstances are.

—Abraham Lincoln

The term "psychopath" started to be used widely during the 1960s, although the first book on the subject, *The Mask of Sanity* by Hervey Cleckley, was published in 1941. It has been in print more or less ever since then. The term "psychopath" has been discussed and debated for decades, and I'm not going to use more words than necessary to explain why that is. The term is generally accepted, though sometimes it is used incorrectly. A lot of people simply use it to refer to people they don't like—*that damned psychopath*—but that is a bit too simplistic. Unfortunately, this common usage means that the term "psychopath" has been so watered down that we sometimes forget that real psychopaths actually exist. In the 1970s, in Sweden, the term itself was seen as stigmatizing, so instead, psychologists and therapists chose to use the expression *in need of special care*. This euphemism was totally crazy—more about that later—so in the 1980s they went back to calling psychopaths by their proper name. Other modern euphemisms are suggested all the time, but it would be dangerous to hide the behavior of the psychopath behind a fancy word that nobody understands. Throughout this book, I have chosen to use the term "psychopath" or "psychopaths."

Psychopaths are without doubt a danger to everybody else around them and for all of society in general. They are wolves disguised as ponies. ("Wolf in sheep's clothing" is rather worn out, don't you think?)

Robert D. Hare, one of the most respected researchers on the subject, has been active in the field since the 1960s and is without doubt a leading expert. He has traveled throughout the world, lectured about psychopaths for almost fifty years, and created a checklist of psychopathic behavior. His opinion is very clear: psychopaths exist, and there are a lot more of them than most of us are aware of.

But are they really a problem?

Psychopathy is at least as common as schizophrenia. The difference is that what the psychopaths do is generally much worse than what people with schizophrenia do. The consequences of psychopaths' ravaging are considerable. In my opinion, they are guilty of lots of risky business deals, lonely-hearts racketeering, swindles and frauds, robberies and organized crime, and drug selling. But also enormous suffering as a result of an endless march of violent wars, lots of murders and ill treatment, rapes, pedophilia, child abuse, torture, and human trafficking.

I am also personally convinced that there are a large number of psychopaths in very high positions in the governments of many countries, in all parts of the world. Very high up in military commands, too, without a doubt. For psychopaths, status and power are of extreme importance, and *if* you can make your way to the top, then why not try to get there?

The majority of psychopaths do not commit obvious crimes, but they are here in our midst, living like everyone else except behind a mask of normality. And we haven't even mentioned the individuals who have managed to convince millions of people that they are in direct contact with higher beings that will punish us if we don't obey: the Messengers. Think about the people from bygone days who convinced parents to bury their children alive in the foundations of their houses to appease the gods. If that isn't manipulation, then I don't know what is.

Tinfoil hats on! somebody might be shouting now. *You're starting to sound like a conspiracy theorist.* I understand what you're getting at, but just stay with me and let's see what you think after you've read more on the subject.

If you haven't given much thought to the term "psychopaths," you'll have something to think about. So many people with such duplicitous behavior? Is it possible? But if it's true, it does explain some of the darkness in the world.

Look around you. It's been a long time since we lived in such troubled times.

There is a lot of material to digest if you want to learn about this type of personality disorder, and at the end of the book I have added a list of books to read if you want to delve deeper. My goal is to give you sufficient knowledge so that you will know when you are the target of a person (or persons) with psychopathic traits and, above all, to give you the knowledge you need to protect yourself.

Even if you are not a sheep, or a pony, the day the wolves invade your pen, you need to be realistic about your chances of escaping without injury. However dramatic this may sound, everyday psychopaths are active with a single goal: to take advantage of any situation for themselves.

Here are a few short explanations of what each item on the psychopathy checklist means:

CHARACTERISTICS	Never (+0 points)	Sometimes (+1 points)	Always (+2 points)
1. Glib and superficial charm	☐	☐	☐
2. Grandiose (exaggeratedly high) estimation of self	☐	☐	☐
3. Lack of remorse or guilt	☐	☐	☐
4. Callousness and lack of empathy	☐	☐	☐
5. Pathological lying	☐	☐	☐
6. Cunning and manipulativeness	☐	☐	☐
7. Shallow affect (superficial emotional responsiveness)	☐	☐	☐
8. Impulsivity	☐	☐	☐
9. Poor behavioral controls	☐	☐	☐
10. Need for stimulation	☐	☐	☐
11. Irresponsibility	☐	☐	☐
12. Early behavioral problems	☐	☐	☐
13. Antisocial behavior as an adult	☐	☐	☐
14. Parasitic lifestyle	☐	☐	☐
15. Sexual promiscuity	☐	☐	☐
16. Lack of realistic long-term goals	☐	☐	☐
17. Failure to accept responsibility for own actions	☐	☐	☐
18. Juvenile delinquency	☐	☐	☐
19. Breaking parole	☐	☐	☐
20. Criminal versatility	☐	☐	☐
TOTAL:	_____	_____	_____
GRAND TOTAL:	_____		

1. GLIB AND SUPERFICIAL CHARM

Psychopaths often have an astoundingly large vocabulary. Many of them talk very fast, and you won't always be able to keep up with their ideas. They are charming, smile a lot, hand out compliments, and make themselves almost ridiculously popular by flattering those they meet. Despite the fact that what they say is often completely illogical and incoherent, they make us believe it is true.

2. GRANDIOSE (EXAGGERATEDLY HIGH) ESTIMATION OF SELF

They think they are better than everyone. They are worth more, deserve greater success in life, than anybody else. Many psychopaths are classic narcissists—that is, they only love themselves. They can boast about real or imagined successes just as easily as ordering a cup of coffee. They also believe they are above all laws—except their own.

3. LACK OF REMORSE OR GUILT

Psychopaths are basically unable to feel remorse. They can pretend to be remorseful when it suits them, but it is never reflected in their actions. It doesn't bother them if they hurt other people. It doesn't matter if it's their worst enemy or their own children. Only they themselves matter.

4. CALLOUSNESS AND LACK OF EMPATHY

Psychopaths know that you feel *something*, but aren't interested in what it is. They can see a seriously injured person and think, "Oh, how interesting." But it doesn't move them, and most psychopaths prefer it like that. They pride themselves on being unaffected by the "personality disorder" of empathy, because it's so much simpler to mistreat or deceive.

5. PATHOLOGICAL LYING

Lying is like breathing. It doesn't require any effort at all. Psychopaths are not embarrassed in the slightest by being caught lying. They can change track before you can bat an eyelid, and will claim that they never said that. It was just a misunderstanding. They will even lie when there is no reason to do so, simply because it is entertaining to deceive others.

6. CUNNING AND MANIPULATIVENESS

Psychopaths "read" other people's weaknesses with alarming ease. And psychopaths turn those weaknesses against their victims for the purpose of deceiving and cheating them. Walking over people is in their nature. They are completely indifferent to the feelings of others, which makes them skilled manipulators. Since they are not worried about being discovered, they take enormous risks and behave so boldly that it's hard to believe that we are being deceived.

7. SHALLOW AFFECT (SUPERFICIAL EMOTIONAL RESPONSIVENESS)

Their emotions aren't really there. No fear, no horror, no worry, no remorse—nothing. Their emotional poverty is total. This isn't something to pity them for, because they are often extremely pleased to avoid feeling when they scheme and deceive. But note that psychopaths can very readily *pretend* to have these emotions.

8. IMPULSIVITY

They live in the present. No planning for the future. If they suddenly have the impulse to eat, they eat. They don't spend any time weighing advantages against disadvantages. The idea of analyzing consequences doesn't exist, which makes them vulnerable. A normal person would likely understand what happens if you beat up somebody on the street, but psychopaths don't think like that. And those with the worst impulse control are indeed locked up in jail.

9. POOR BEHAVIORAL CONTROLS

Even though they subject those around them to dreadful abuses, they themselves are very easily offended. The slightest mistake or rash comment can result in a violent attack of fury if they consider it a prov-ocation. When violent, psychopaths attack physically; otherwise, some verbal assault will come down on the person who happened to open their mouth at the wrong time. The strange thing is that the anger dis-appears immediately afterward. As if there was an on–off switch.

10. NEED FOR STIMULATION

They need their dopamine kicks. Excitement and arousal are great. If they can't do crazy things themselves, they try to get others to do them. When the rest of us get nervous if we see a police car and immediately check the speedometer, psychopaths often start revving the engine. All for the sake of excitement.

11. IRRESPONSIBILITY

They never take responsibility for anything. Resolving debts, pay-ing child support, protecting themselves when having casual sex—the psychopath stands above all that. They don't care, and often get away with it because the world is full of other people who do care. A true psychopath doesn't even take responsibility for their own children, even though they claim to love them. They can easily leave them alone for a very long time without food or water.

12. EARLY BEHAVIORAL PROBLEMS

Most psychopaths exhibit deviant behavior before the age of twelve. This can be anything from cruelty to animals and toward other children to stealing and lying without the slightest concern. Very early sexual experiences also occur, and there are examples of twelve-year-olds who have committed rape.

13. ANTISOCIAL BEHAVIOR AS AN ADULT

A true psychopath doesn't care about society's norms. The rules that apply to the rest of us don't apply to them. Such rules limit their freedom to do whatever they want, so they make up their own rules. It's not uncommon that this is the reason some of them end up behind bars.

14. PARASITIC LIFESTYLE

Psychopaths believe that their splendid qualities give them the right to live off of others. They never pay the bills if they can get someone else to do it. They often have debts and owe taxes because little details like income tax and bill due dates bore them. They never offer to pay at the restaurant (they will always forget their wallet), and they are happy to borrow money from family and friends without ever paying it back. If they are called out, they simply blame somebody else.

15. SEXUAL PROMISCUITY

Psychopaths often have numerous short-lived sexual interactions. Their charm attracts many people, so they are never short of a partner. And permanent infidelity keeps things interesting, while at the same time it is exciting for them to deceive their partner. How much can the psychopath get away with?

16. LACK OF REALISTIC LONG-TERM GOALS

If you live in the "here and now," you don't need any long-term plan. Psychopaths don't plan anything: planning is something completely contrary to their impulsive preference. Quite often they become a sort of nomad who changes partners and jobs as the mood strikes them. They never look forward or back. The aim is to live life at the expense of others, and that takes no planning at all.

17. FAILURE TO ACCEPT RESPONSIBILITY FOR OWN ACTIONS

Whatever they have done, they will never admit it. Even if they were caught on camera doing something, they will deny it. A psychopath always has somebody else to blame. Even if they understand that they have done something wrong, they'll name a scapegoat. They are even amused by watching someone else take the blame for what they themselves have done.

18. JUVENILE DELINQUENCY

It is very common for psychopaths to have had problems with the law early in life. Because psychopathy often begins to show itself clearly at around ten years of age, they can cause quite a lot of trouble when they're young. The fact that fifteen-year-olds commit rape, assault, robbery, and even murder should definitely be regarded as abnormal.

19. BREAKING PAROLE

Yet again, ordinary rules don't apply to psychopaths. And punishments don't work either. They don't react to ordinary threats of repercussions, because they lack the ability to consider the consequences of their actions. This means that they will often do whatever they want once they are released.

20. CRIMINAL VERSATILITY

While other criminals specialize in one thing, such as robbing security vans, mugging, assault, or perhaps narcotics, psychopaths are much more versatile. In a sense, they are curious, and they try everything.

So How Does the List Work?
Who Does It Apply To?

The list has twenty derangements, each of which is ranked from 0 to 2, depending on whether the trait occurs always, sometimes, or never for a given individual. If, for example, the person we are examining never shows any sign of narcissism, then they will get no points under that item. If there are some clear but inconsistent signs of narcissism, they would score one point. But if this character trait is evident virtually all the time, they would score two points. This means that up to 40 points can be scored. Well-known psychopaths such as Charles Manson and certain serial killers usually score 35–40 points, but in Robert Hare's opinion, you should be on your guard around a person with a score of 15–20 points. Such a person does not have good intentions. If you should meet somebody who scores thirty points or more, then you should definitely think about your situation, and do so damned quickly. You are facing a really serious problem, and in the worst case the psychopath is somebody who is far too close to you.

Hmm, I Recognize Myself . . . and My Partner . . . and My Boss

In assessing your own behavior, you will certainly be able to tick some of the items on the list above 0. Does that make you a psychopath? Of course not. There are a lot of people who exhibit certain psychopathic traits but not others, but without connection to *other* psychopathic traits, and that doesn't make them psychopaths in a clinical sense. But, naturally, the more items that are scored above 0 on the list, the worse it is for those around the person.

There are lots of impulsive people: many are charming, and some talk like machine guns. That doesn't make them psychopaths. There are serial killers who aren't psychopaths either. Many of them suffer from mental illness, but that is something completely different.

But isn't this a kind of mental illness? Shouldn't we feel sorry for psychopaths?

Psychopaths are not psychotic or mentally ill. "Psychotic" is a psychological term that means the brain is in an abnormal condition.

It is used for a serious, but *temporary*, mental condition. Some illnesses that can lead to a psychosis are schizophrenia, schizoaffective disorder, and delusional disorder. Bipolar type 1 disorder and severe depressions can also include psychotic symptoms.

Psychopathy, however, is termed a personality disorder, so it is not a mental disorder or mental illness. Psychopathy is regarded as largely having genetic causes, but unfavorable childhood conditions and earlier brain damage can sometimes play a part. A mental disorder means that a person feels so bad that it causes a considerable degree of suffering for the person themselves: mentally, socially, and perhaps economically.

A mental disorder or illness can manifest itself in many different ways. Some mental disorders are socially disabling because they are clearly visible in behavior or speech, so the person affected is prevented from giving "full expression" to their personality. The disorder is classified from the point of view of the person with the disorder, how they experience difficulties and suffering. The classification also takes into consideration the affected person's self-awareness and understanding of real life. This distinction is important for understanding the difference between psychopathy and mental illness.

In contrast to someone affected by a mental disorder, a psychopath does not feel that they are ill. In fact, they feel great and consider themselves to be mentally stable. (They can, however, simulate illness if it serves their purpose.) They didn't become psychopaths because they were bullied in school. Nor are they maladjusted unfortunates who didn't know better when they made a total mess of things for you. They are abnormal by your and my standards, but at the same time *fully aware of what they do*. In their own eyes, they are simply higher up on the food chain than everybody else.

So What if a Few of the Things on the List Apply to Me? Am I a Psychopath?

The difference between you and a psychopath is that you have a moral sense. You feel with all your body what is right and what is wrong. And you care about others. You do not consciously want to hurt anybody around you. Should you happen to do so, you will presumably feel bad about it. This—among many other factors—is what makes you human.

The psychopath doesn't feel anything. They do what they want to do, since their base assumption is that they have that right. They know that they risk ending up in prison for some of their actions, but that doesn't stop them. According to their logic, they aren't going to get caught. Instead, they coldly take the risk and assume that they will get away with it. And should they get caught, they will probably have already worked out how they can pin the blame on somebody else for what they've done. The psychopath would blame their own brother without batting an eye if doing so would help get them off the hook. They are not affected by your suffering and don't care if you end up completely broke or lose your job because of them. They lack all remorse and never look back.

A psychopath counts on the fact that they appear normal in behavior and appearance. But they carry out their actions with cold-blooded, calculating intellect. They think, but they don't feel. They do exactly what a wolf does when it wants a sheep. They take it.

If you haven't previously read about true psychopathy, I understand that you might feel rather dubious about the whole thing. Do people like this really exist? Unfortunately, they do.

There Are More Than You Think

Robert Hare concludes that at least 2 percent of the population in the industrialized world would score so highly on the psychopathy checklist that they would be classified as psychopaths. More recently, John Clarke, the author of *Working with Monsters,* indicates that the figure is higher: Something like 6 percent of the male population and about 2 percent of the female population are probably psychopaths (indeed, most figures indicate that the disorder is more common among men). The Swedish psychologist Sigvard Lingh has written several very well-informed books on psychopathy, and he is of the opinion that the percentage of the population that is psychopathic has long been 4–5 percent. But in his most recent book, *Everyday Psychopaths,* he has suggested that the figure may be even higher.

There are variations in the percentage of psychopaths in different parts of the world. For some reason, there seems to be a higher percentage of psychopaths in the United States than in Great Britain, for example. One speculation is that American society more strongly rewards self-centered behavior than does British society. If I were to base my calculations on the lower estimate (2 percent), it would mean that there are about seven million psychopaths in what is called the largest democracy in the world, the USA. In Sweden, we get away with about 200,000 psychopaths.

Real-Life Psychopaths

Everyday psychopathic behavior is all around us. While I was writing this particular chapter, I heard about the following example from some distant acquaintances.

An elderly man, an old bachelor, met a woman with five adult children. They got married and enjoyed each other's company, and he lived to a surprisingly ripe old age. When he finally succumbed, it happened that he was rather well-off. The woman inherited over a million dollars. Slightly embarrassed by her sudden wealth, she decided to divide up the inheritance into six equal parts. One part for her, and the other five parts to her five adult children. Within the space of three months, one of her sons had swindled his mother out of her share and three of the other four siblings out of their shares. The fifth sibling, the oldest sister, who turned out to be immune to psychopaths (there is an exclusive group of people who actually are immune, and psychopaths usually try to get rid of them to remove the threat they pose), refused to "lend" the money to her brother. In response, he threatened her with extreme violence. But since the sister had long since seen through him, she still refused to hand over a single cent. He more or less shrugged his shoulders and disappeared with the money from his mother and other siblings. Nobody in the family has heard of him since then, and the money has vanished, just as he has.

You won't read about this type of case very often in the newspapers. It is a bit like domestic violence. The victims are ashamed and rarely report the incidents. Since many psychopaths deceive close family and friends—the victims who are easiest to target and pose the least risk for psychopaths—they remain undetected and can continue.

This pattern is very common. Psychopaths have a parasitic lifestyle. They enjoy eating at nice restaurants, but it will always be you who foots the bill.

I know. You're thinking: *That's just so embarrassing! To never pay your share! What will people say?* Yes, what will people say? You're thinking like a normal person. Stop doing that. You can't use ordinary logic in these contexts. The psychopath thinks they have the right to commit these transgressions since they stand above all the rest of us.

2

Protecting Yourself: A Basic Defense Against Psychopaths

A lie told often enough becomes the truth.
—Vladimir Ilyich Lenin

You can take measures to help protect you from predatory people. If you are already in the clutches of a psychopath, then it might be too late. You will need enormous mental strength to break out from his or her hold. However, there are three preventative steps you can take:

1. Increase your self-awareness.
2. Learn how to recognize psychopathic behavior.
3. Decide how much you value your own worth and self-respect.

That sounds fairly simple, doesn't it? Knowledge is definitely power here. The more you know about how psychopathy expresses itself, the stronger your defense against manipulation will be.

Let's take a closer look at these three points and why they are important.

1. Increase Your Self-Awareness

Everyone here who is 100 percent self-aware—hands up! Anybody? No? Exactly. If you function normally and are not a psychopath yourself, you realize that there are things about yourself that you might not understand. This applies to all of us: we have blind spots and behave in ways we don't understand. Sometimes this isn't a big deal, but on other occasions we can exhibit unexpected behaviors—for example, if we find ourselves threatened. No one knows with certainty how they will react until they are standing with a weapon aimed at them.

It's sometimes said that psychopaths don't understand or are unable to imagine the feelings of others. Nothing could be more incorrect. On the contrary, research shows that they understand perfectly how you feel in certain situations. The problem is that the psychopaths *themselves* don't feel anything and therefore completely ignore your emotions. They expose your weak points extremely quickly. Once they know your weaknesses, they will use them ruthlessly. Your best defense is to be extremely watchful of those who seem to focus their attentions on your weak points. You need to be far more cautious in your evaluation of these people. (This is difficult because they will not begin a relationship by looking for the chinks in your armor. They'll start somewhere else entirely. But more about this later.)

If you are susceptible to flattery, it will show. It's incredibly simple to test if this is the case. Just let someone give you a bit of unexpected praise and see how you react. You might blush or start giggling. If you recognize yourself in this, then you are a walking invitation to confidence tricksters of every possible type.

People who take shortcuts in life, who don't have any problem being in the moral "gray zone," are especially vulnerable to psychopaths and their shady plans. People with a strong desire to earn quick money are tricked every minute by skilled swindlers who promise them the moon and the stars.

But, of course, it isn't always so easy to know who you are or to recognize that you might be easily flattered or swindled. But even you have weak points, dear reader. There are no perfect people. In the book *Surrounded by Idiots,* I gave a thorough description of the DISC system, and some of that will be repeated here soon, but it's one thing to read about behavioral types and quite another to apply that information.

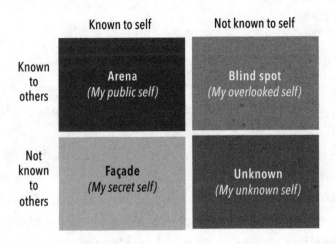

The Johari Window

The Johari window is a psychological model that is used to characterize different ways of communicating. The model was developed in the 1950s at the University of California by psychologists Joseph Luft and Harrington Ingham. (The name Johari is formed from a combination of their two first names.) The model describes how openness in interpersonal communication increases when we both act as unique individuals and are simultaneously aware of the people and relationships around us. Giving each other feedback is an important process in all forms of cooperation. By being able to receive feedback, by being sensitive, I am able to gain insight into how other people see me and my actions. At the same time, by being unique and being brave enough to expose my true self, I give others the opportunity to gain knowledge about me.

The public self (open or arena quadrant) comprises what I know about myself and what others know about me. If that quadrant gets larger, it means that openness increases. This takes place when my exposure—how I share my unique inner self with others—increases at the same time that my sensitivity for others increases. When I start making use of my strengths and dare to learn about my weaknesses, the public self grows.

The overlooked self (blind-spot quadrant) is formed by what I don't know about myself but others do know about me. This information can be learned from things I say that others notice, but that I myself am unaware of—for instance, expressions or turns of phrase I use too often.

The secret self (façade quadrant) is formed by what I know about myself but which others do not know about me. This self-knowledge can include things I don't have the slightest intention of sharing or showing to anybody. But if a person hides too much of themselves from others, the façade quadrant becomes larger.

The unknown self (unknown quadrant) consists of what I don't know about myself and what others don't know about me. The parts of the personality found here are shrouded in mystery for everybody and might only come out under extreme pressure.

According to the theory, people with a large open quadrant—that is, a large public self that they share with the world—have the best chance of being able to communicate with others, because their open manner facilitates communication. The result is that the people around them are less likely to misunderstand them or incorrectly interpret their statements and actions. Openness and, with it, communication between people are optimized when both sensitivity to the feelings of others and a willingness to share about yourself are equally large. Then the open window is at its maximum.

Of course, it's not always desirable to have a large open quadrant. With occasional and superficial acquaintances, for example, it's not especially meaningful. What is the point of letting strangers know your innermost thoughts? (Though there are many people who do precisely that.)

Other people will not view your behavior in the same way, nor will they necessarily view you the way you view yourself. Some things are invisible to others because you choose not to show them. But sometimes others—for example, your colleagues at work—will actually notice things about you that you are totally unaware of. And before you exclaim that this is just because they've completely misunderstood you, I'm going to tell you that it doesn't matter. Communication is dependent on the recipient. When the recipient has filtered the message though their frame of reference, prejudices, and experiences, what remains is what they understand. Regardless of what you actually meant.

Blind Spots

To express this using DISC language: a Red person thinks they are clever and have drive, but those around them also see that they are sometimes tense and impolite. A Yellow person readily calls attention to their creative and innovative sides, while their coworkers are busy tidying up after their unfinished projects. While the Green does everything so that their colleagues will be comfortable and thus fetches coffee for everyone who wants it, their boss sees that they back down in potential conflicts—even when they're right. And the Blue perfectionist gets on the nerves of everyone around them because of their inability to let go of any detail that is not 100 percent correct. What others see as pathological pedantry, the Blue person sees as performing quality work.

Who is right, and who is wrong? It doesn't matter in the slightest. It's simply the way things are. If you're going to claim that you have absolute self-awareness, then you have to admit you have weaknesses. And, as I've described, individuals with a hidden agenda have a very keen nose for your weaknesses. You won't be completely protected from being manipulated unless you accept that you're not perfect and are prepared to deal with your less flattering sides.

My Own Shortcomings—Listen Carefully!

Personally, I dislike talking about my own weaknesses. It's a lot nicer to talk about my successes and soak up the praise from my loved ones. But the weaknesses are there nevertheless.

In my case it's about impulsiveness (Red behavior), which means that I can make decisions without having thought them through. This is a tendency that has, for example, cost me a great deal in the form of losses on the stock market, expensive repairs of old cars that were supposedly in "good condition," and thoughtless comments to people that I care deeply about, when I was really only trying to be funny.

And on the subject of being funny: Historically I have often used humor at the wrong times (Yellow behavior). I have learned to control these impulses better nowadays, but I can easily rattle off a list of the occasions when I've made a mess of a situation by not taking it seriously. Sometimes I can be careless about details even though I know full well how important they are. And we haven't even mentioned being a time optimist, interrupting others because what I have to say is so much more interesting, or being grumpy when somebody points out any of the failings I've written about in this paragraph.

And I do, undoubtedly, have a definite strain of perfectionism (Blue behavior). For example, it is still extremely hard for me to give a lecture without going through the material just one more time, polishing up some of the pictures, and making something sound better. Even though I have lectured for more than twenty years, I can't refrain from doing this. (Or when I put in some new plants in the garden, I can't just drop them in any old way; first, I must look at the installation from nineteen different angles before I even touch a shovel. And, yes, most people wonder what on earth I am doing.) When I talk with people, I can sometimes be so focused that I'm practically scowling with concentration, or so I have been told. Oh, dear.

Well, there you have it. It wasn't so bad, was it? Now you know a little more about me, and none of the examples I've given are particularly flattering. These are things I struggle with, and I often wish that I was different in these areas. Does that make me a bad person? I don't think so. I'm human. Just like you, and just like everybody else I've met. We all have flaws we regret. As I've grown older—I've just passed fifty as I write this—it has become easier to admit that I'm not perfect. After having worked with human behavior for a couple of decades, I've learned lots of things, including about myself. But, nevertheless, there are still patterns in my own behavior that I'm not aware of. Traits and actions that others see but I am blind to.

So what about you?

If *I* can acknowledge my weaknesses, then *you* too can do the same. See it as a chance to be better; to improve yourself; to be more easily accepted by those around you, if you think that's important; to achieve your goals more quickly. So take a piece of paper and a pen. You know what you should do now.

When you've finished, you can always just eat the paper so that it won't fall into the wrong hands. But I would really, genuinely, and seriously ask you to sit and consider your weak points. Learn what they are and work on strengthening them. And, above all, be wary of people who seem to target them. Because there are people who actively search for openings.

2. Learn How to Recognize Psychopathic Behavior

What is the difference between psychopaths and people with psychopathic traits? Remember, to be classified as a psychopath you need to exhibit a sufficient number of the psychopathic behaviors named on Robert D. Hare's psychopathy checklist.

Some items on the list are not, on their own, particularly alarming. *Glib and superficial charm*. That fits a lot of people. Most Yellow people can tick off that item. Or *impulsivity*. Fairly typical Red behavior. If you think it, you do it and then see how it goes. *Irresponsibility?* Well, it isn't unusual for Green people to back away when responsibility is being given out. And that's mainly because responsibility is far too much work. So we can see that certain psychopathic behaviors can be found in all sorts of people. I myself can tick off a couple of behaviors, perhaps even three or four on the list. However, if you find a considerable number of these behaviors in one person, then there is reason to be very cautious.

Sorry to be blunt, but there is no other way of putting it. Just as the wolf, when hungry, doesn't care about how afraid or injured the sheep get, a full-fledged psychopath doesn't care the slightest about you. You are simply prey, nothing else. Just like the sheep farmer has to learn how to keep the wolves away, you must learn how to recognize a psychopath.

Even if you still think that the threat of psychopaths probably isn't that big of an issue, I would like to point out the following: According to the statistics, the risk of being affected by a psychopath is greater than the risk of:

- Having a heart attack
- Being diagnosed with cancer
- Smashing your thumb with a hammer

- Crashing your car
- Being robbed in town on a Friday night
- Becoming an alcoholic
- Losing all your pension funds in the stock market
- Getting sacked from your job

Nonetheless, we work to protect ourselves from all of the above in our everyday lives. We eat nourishing food, don't drink too much, use seatbelts, and don't walk home alone on a Friday night. We do our jobs well so as not to be made redundant the next time they make staff cuts. But we do *nothing* to protect ourselves from psychopaths—probably because we don't want to believe that they represent a real threat to us, if we even fathom that they exist at all.

We're not talking about Hannibal Lecter here. As I noted in the introduction, we are talking about someone who could very easily be sitting just two desks away from you and who smiles at you every morning.

Don't be naïve. See the danger before it sees you.

3. Decide How Much You Value Your Own Worth and Self-Respect

What has this got to do with self-respect? Answer: absolutely everything. If you think that you deserve the best in life, then you ought to ensure that you get it. And now I am not talking about this the way a psychopath would. I'm asking you to consider how important it is to you to retain a sound and healthy level of respect for yourself, your self-awareness, and your image of who you are.

Do you consider yourself a good person? Do you think that, despite your faults and shortcomings, you should be loved and able to enjoy life, however it might turn out? This is not a book designed to help you build your self-confidence, but I think self-confidence is exactly what you deserve. Everyone deserves to be loved. That's my philosophy.

Nevertheless, many of us have problems with this. Our self-esteem is too low because we don't like who we are. We are dissatisfied with ourselves: We wish that we were younger, older, slimmer, more attractive, wealthier, more clever at this or that or that we had a more interesting partner or could speak French. Regardless of the specific dissatisfactions, we too often feel dissatisfied with the person we are. And that makes us easy prey for psychopaths or people with psychopathic traits.

In a sense, psychopaths are incredibly cowardly. They really do act like the wolf when it eventually manages to get inside the pen. They rarely attack the alpha—the strongest animal in the pen—because they're not certain they can win. But wounded prey? The one that's had a rough time in life? Undoubtedly. They pounce on the weakest member of the flock. The slow ones, the ones that look a bit droopy and show some sign of weakness. In the case of humans, the weakest member of the flock is the person who doesn't like themselves. That person will always be easily influenced by, for example, flattery. If you don't think that anybody can love you, terrible as you are, then you'll be willing to invite in anybody who shows you the slightest appreciation.

You don't think this can happen to you? Okay, but you do know that such people are out there and that less watchful friends of yours might find themselves in trouble. Perhaps this knowledge can give you the opportunity to support and help those friends.

Your task is to accept who you are. By all means, work on your shortcomings and try to develop yourself in all areas. Learn how you function and think about what strengths you want to have. At the same time, you can reflect upon weaknesses that you want to turn into strengths. That is a positive approach that gives you energy and makes you a more complete individual. But don't deny who you are.

Like yourself.

Love yourself.

Realize that you don't need anybody else to do just that. Develop yourself because *you* want to—not because somebody is picking on you.

And I want to conclude with the following: Being independent and on your own does *not* make you strong. The wolf singles out one of the sheep from the flock before it rips it to pieces. Make sure that the psychopath doesn't single you out and isolate you from your loved ones. You can find examples of this later on in the book. Get help from your family or your friends if you suspect that you have a problem ahead of you.

Right. Now you have three ways to help protect yourself.

3

Who Are the Psychopaths?

If you don't control your mind, someone else will.

—John Allston

Research definitively shows that the majority of human decisions are based on emotional, not rational, factors. How much logic do we really use when we do make a decision? Often, something just feels damned good and so we do it. Afterward, we can't always explain why we did what we did. It just felt like a good idea at the time.

INFORMATION	INFLUENCE
20% of our decisions are based on rational analysis	80% of our decisions are based on emotional convictions

Just think about it. The last time you spent a large sum of money: Was it for rational, logical reasons, or was it because it felt right? Some jewelry, a car, a house? This morning before I began writing, I looked at cars online. One of Sweden's cheapest cars is called a Dacia. I don't know much about cars, but it looks like a fairly simple car without a lot of extras: a little engine, good gas mileage, and the cost of insurance on it is cheap. I'm sure that it's quite satisfactory if you mainly drive short distances. It would probably be a fairly rational decision to buy such a car. I've never actually met anybody who owns this sensible little car. But I do have lots of acquaintances who drive a BMW, Mercedes, Lexus, or a similarly expensive car. "Safety," they usually exclaim, somewhat offended, when I wonder why they spent so much money on a car. And, of course, safety is important. But a Volvo, which doesn't cost nearly as much as a Lexus, is undoubtedly just as safe. The feel-good decision-making wins out over the rational side again.

Is there any difference between small and big decisions?

But what about a house? Now we're talking big money. You really do need to think rationally with this kind of investment; otherwise, everything can go wrong. With such large amounts of money, you can't let your heart choose because a wrong decision can have severe consequences. If you ruin your finances by paying too much for a house, you risk ruining your marriage, too. As a former bank official, I have seen more than one family fall apart because they couldn't pay their bills. So when you buy a house, you have to be rational. That's what most people do, right?

On the other hand: Have you ever been to a viewing with a real estate agent? Gotten out of your car, looked up the gravel drive, looked around the garden, and already said to your partner: *This is it! This is home!*

A lot of people I talk to about house buying claim that this isn't the case. *You see*, they say in a friendly voice but with a face that implies I've missed the point, *you have to go to the bank, do your sums, work out interest rates and repayments. There's an awful lot of logic and information behind a decision!*

Indeed!

But at the same time, if the estimate of your living costs and mortgage plan (and interest rates) is optimistic, are you going to give up your dream house? Don't we try to convince that severe-looking bank official that we'll sell the second car, and who actually needs a boat nowadays?

To save time, let's admit to each other that we aren't particularly good at making totally rational decisions. We are emotional beings. We let our feelings lead us along. And I think this is perfectly all right. But it is also the reason why some people are so clever at manipulating others.

Some people are better at using their influence than others. That's what makes them good sellers. They've found the key to other people's emotions. That doesn't necessarily mean that they're clever manipulators (although that might very well be the case), but it does mean that they know how to lead us to where they want us to go. Sometimes, it really is fortuitous—perhaps I hadn't understood the value of proposal X, and now I meet someone who takes off my blinders and shows me the opportunity. But regardless of what the purpose is, it's good for you to understand how you are influenced by various individuals you meet.

So Who Are the Manipulators? The Usual Suspects Are . . .

Who are these manipulative and exploitative people? They are the people who find it easy to use your emotions. This often means that the ones who know you best end up on the list of possible candidates. Even if you shouldn't start suspecting all the members of your family and close friends, I would like to point out the areas of greatest risk. Of course, this doesn't mean that you should start looking askance at everyone close to you, but neither should you be blind to reality. Knowledge is power. You obviously don't need to worry about people you already know personally and who aren't trying to trick you into doing things you don't want to do. But when new people enter your life, you should at first regard them with open eyes. Don't mistrust them, but observe them a little more than you usually do. Be clear-eyed without becoming paranoid.

These are the people who can most easily get at you:

- Members of your family
- Your husband/wife or live-in partner
- Romantic or sexual partner
- Relationships at your place of work: your boss, your coworkers, or your subordinates
- Friends and acquaintances
- Professional contacts: doctors, lawyers, psychologists, or others you might turn to for help

Oh, dear! you might be thinking now. *That covers virtually everyone I know.* That's the bad news. Psychopaths look just the same as the rest of us, and they are all related to somebody. But what counts is whether a relationship gives you something: strength, friendship, joy, love, or economic gain. If it does, then of course it is positive. But if the relationship hurts you by stealing your peace of mind, your money, your faith in the future, or in life itself, then it's time to do something about it.

The Ones You'll Never Have to Meet

Then, of course, we have the classic manipulators that you'll never actually meet. History is absolutely littered with them—tyrannical rulers who made entire nations cower. Hitler manipulated an entire people to start a world conflagration. Terrorists have made us get undressed in front of strangers at airports. Fanatics manipulate children to blow themselves up for something that no human has ever seen. The financial markets are populated by skilled manipulators who make us open our wallets and invest money in projects we can't even begin to understand. Some of the things that happen around us make me seriously wonder how many psychopaths there are in incredibly high positions in all fields. If you look at what goes on around us, you can't help but come to certain conclusions.

But these individuals are too distant for us to deal with. We can't do anything about the fact that the world is partly governed through manipulation and, in some cases, severe psychopathy. But we can keep our own backyard nice and clean.

In this book, I have chosen to devote attention to two primary suspects: your partner, and your colleagues at work. Okay, your boss, too. Perhaps especially him or her. Here are a few things to bear in mind before we move on.

Your Psychopathic Partner

If your partner is a psychopath, it's very unfortunate. Even if they swear absolute loyalty and love in front of everyone at the altar, they are simply a person who has learned to say the right words. They have seen how it's done in the movies and, since they are skilled actors, have no difficulty playing along. True emotions are totally unfathomable to them, but they know what such emotions should look like. They have trained themselves to say the right words. They most likely pinched the marriage vows from the internet and have learned which words will bring tears to your eyes. Unfortunately, they don't mean any of what they say; this is simply part of a larger plan.

The psychopath has no intention of fulfilling their grandiose promises; rather, they are very pleased that they've managed to con you so well. How can you be so stupid and gullible? You just got married to a wolf, but you don't know it yet. But trust me when I say that they are going to enjoy all the pickings at your smorgasbord.

Because that is exactly what a psychopath does. They don't marry or live with you because they love you or respect you. *So why do they do it?* you might be wondering. To own you and all your belongings and assets. They will drain you of everything. It might take a few years, and they will look like the perfect partner for a while. They will charm your relatives and your friends and do everything to build up a picture of themselves as the dream partner. They will help with things, offer to take on tasks—which you will very likely end up doing yourself—and stake out their territory. And if you start complaining, they can point to all the outsiders who think they are a dream partner. The people who have never seen their dark side.

But psychopaths can't act the part of the perfect partner very long. They get bored of being the pretend person they have created to en-snare you. Because it wasn't an actual person at all.

The psychopath will then move ahead with their main plan: to leech off you until you are no longer steady on your feet. Instead of growing old together with you, they will make you old before your time. There are examples of psychopathic partners who have taken the expression "until death do us part" very literally—as the ulti-mate escape plan. But when all your money has gone, when the house has been mortgaged for more than it's worth, when you have used all your credit cards to their limit and can't give a penny more, they'll move on to the next victim.

The psychopath believes that everything of yours is theirs, and everything of theirs is theirs. Their grandiosity is expressed in their assumption that they have a right to everything. You are simply an asset, nothing more.

The good news is that if you can see the warning signs early on (perhaps after reading this book), then you can adopt countermea-sures. You can refuse to play along. You can say that you saw im-mediately what was happening. If you're not a "good" victim, the psychopath will move on. There are so many gullible people out there; why stick with one who is difficult? And you will have escaped the psychopath's clutches! You are more than that weak person, just asking to be deceived.

Your Psychopathic Coworker

The psychopathic coworker attracts everything and everyone to them by being where everyone else is. You'll find them beside the coffee machine, where they take every opportunity to find new prey. The technique is often used to seduce a new public with their fascinating personality and get people to think that they're fantastic. But this is just one big show. They rarely reveal to anybody who they actually are. In the presence of a psychopath, other coworkers can behave as if they've been drugged. They see nothing other than a person who looks great, who smells good, and who always says exactly the right thing at exactly the right moment.

This person quickly stands out as your best friend, as a reliable and loyal colleague; the person is everything for everybody. When I describe it like this, it seems too good to be true, doesn't it? And it is. The problem is that everybody in the office has been so enchanted by this person that they don't notice the psychopath doesn't do good work. Psychopaths rarely get the best results because they don't do any work if they can get someone else to do it for them. But they are more than willing to take the credit for the successes of other people. They can easily go to the boss and talk about a big deal, which you actually made, and say that they were behind it all. When the rumor finally reaches you, it's sometimes too late to correct it.

Your psychopathic colleague would name and shame you or even accuse you of some made-up blunder without a moment's hesitation if they thought that they could gain something by so doing. If they find your weaknesses, then they will rip into you without blinking. Your livelihood or the reputation of the firm where you work means nothing.

If you lose your job, it would be a pity, of course, but that's your problem. Even if the psychopath has met your family and played with your children, they are capable of stabbing a knife in your back just the same.

The psychopath would not feel the slightest regret about throwing a hand grenade in your direction, letting it explode, and then leaning back with a self-satisfied smirk to observe how the bits of you and your wrecked career fall slowly to the ground. They feel totally disconnected from how your family would be affected by the catastrophe.

I am aware of how vicious this sounds, but I want you to understand how great a threat a psychopath is.

To make it even clearer: Your psychopathic colleague doesn't give a damn about you.

And about smirking: Psychopaths don't smile as often as one might be led to believe. And they laugh rather rarely. Laughter is a spontaneous reaction: You see something you aren't prepared for, and then you burst out laughing because it was funny. And humor works a bit like empathy. You need to understand something about the world and feel something for humor to work. But psychopaths don't know what's so funny. They don't laugh at what we laugh at, and if they try to laugh, it will sound weird. They know that, so they don't. They'll never be the class clown.

If you have a class clown in your office, you don't need to be worried. Such a person can be a bit annoying at times, but they are most likely not a psychopath.

Many psychopaths appear to be the brooding type. They win people's confidence through their affected warmth, not through attracting a large audience to entertain.

Your Psychopathic Boss

Now imagine if your psychopathic colleague isn't your colleague at all . . . but your boss.

Can you imagine what damage they can do?

Kevin Dutton, a British psychologist, has done research showing that psychopaths are more common in the following professions, which give the psychopath power, money, and excitement, as well as the opportunity to control other people and dominate their lives:

1. CEO (interpreted as the highest boss in a firm or company, regardless of whether it is legal or not)
2. lawyer
3. media jobs (TV/radio)
4. sales
5. surgeon
6. journalist
7. police officer
8. religious leader
9. chef
10. civil servant

4

Surrounded by Idiots?

This Is How You Get Rid of Them

I never lie . . . at least not to those I don't love.
—Anne Rice, *The Vampire Lestat*

The best way to protect yourself against psychopaths is by increasing your self-awareness. And that's what we will do now, by exploring the colors and behavior patterns of the DISC system.

Let's take a closer look at how different behavior types can be translated into colors according to the DISC system that I mentioned earlier.

Red, dominant behavior is what you see in extroverted, task-oriented individuals who operate at a fast pace in all aspects of life. They are motivated, forward-looking problem-solvers, intent on getting results and meeting targets. They like activity and soon tire if things stand still too long.

Yellow, influential behavior means happy, creative, extroverted relationship people who communicate easily with everyone. Like Red people, they also like a fast pace; however, they are much more oriented toward the people around them. They get easily bored by too many details.

Green, stable behavior means a more reserved and introverted person. These are people who are oriented toward the happiness of

THE BASIC PILLARS IN DISC

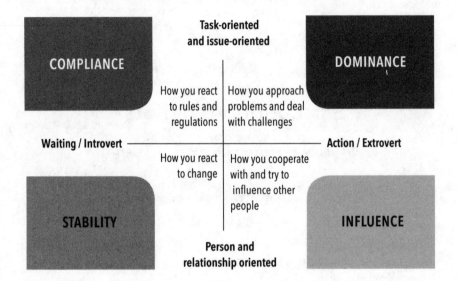

the group and work to ensure that there aren't any conflicts. They like cooperation and are very good listeners.

Blue, compliant behavior means introverted and task-oriented people who like things to be well-ordered and want to work methodically and with structure. They appreciate quality and rarely or never miss any details.

There you have it! Are you an expert now? No, I didn't expect you to be. We need to delve a bit deeper into the various behavior types.

Red (Dominant) Behavior

The Alpha or Super Achiever

The easiest way to recognize a Red person is to look them in the eye. The reason is that they will do something that most people do not: they will meet your gaze without looking away. Most people don't meet your gaze for more than a few seconds before looking away briefly. But Red people like to look a little longer, since they want to see who you are. They are measuring their potential opposition and are behaving in a confrontational manner in this respect. They are ready to simply stare you down.

The next step is the handshake. Firm, perhaps even a bit too firm. Dominant. You are dealing with someone who isn't going to let you walk over them. A consultant I met many years ago had a weird handshake. He took the other person's hand and twisted it slightly so that the back of his own hand ended upward. Then he pushed a little downward to show that he was strongest. This is an extremely dominant way of shaking hands, because it signals that he expects you to be subservient. I don't know whether he was aware of this, but it was very uncomfortable for those on the receiving end.

The first time I shook hands with him, I was so astounded that I didn't do anything. The second time, I was prepared and resisted—which surprised him, so he gripped harder, and I resisted even more firmly. I looked him in the eye and asked what on earth was he doing. Finally, he stopped trying. We never got on very well.

The body language of the Reds also supplies lots of clues. They often have a straight posture and walk rather quickly. They look straight ahead and expect people to get out of the way. Of course, there are exceptions, as always. But it's highly unlikely that you'll come across a listless Red person. They simply don't work like that.

How Do You Recognize a True Alpha?

The Red person often talks relatively quickly and intensely. They don't have a problem raising their voices if it becomes necessary. Correction: if *they* think it's necessary—that is, any time someone doesn't agree with them. Then they repeat the same argument, but louder. These are winner types who like to emphasize everything. The Reds will persist in a discussion even if earlier on in the conversation they realized that they are wrong; since they hate losing, they'll just keep charging ahead at full steam.

Not particularly charming, you might think. The Red person doesn't care. Not being relationship people, they just shrug off the opinions of others. That might actually be their greatest strength: They don't let other people's feelings and opinions steer them too much. They're not completely insensitive—far from it—but they distinguish between a situation and a person.

I came across an example of a Red a couple of years ago in an organization I was working with. The department head wasn't purely Red; he also had a bit of Yellow in him, but the Red traits were strong enough for him to be able to solve the following problem:

> One of the teams was getting very little done. Discipline was poor and morale was low. People came and went as they felt like it, took long lunches, and spent a lot of time surfing the internet during work hours. Very few of the employees on the team took responsibility for anything be-yond their own desks. The team leader had tried to whip the group into shape several times without success. The team was way below its targets and had been for a long time. Out of eight similar teams, their numbers were the worst.

What would you have done if you were head of the department? You would have given some harsh feedback. Which is what happened. The head of the department called that particular team leader in at about eleven in the morning and gave him some feedback on how he was doing with his team. The conversation was predominantly nega-tive, as you would expect.

Since I ended up being the person who sorted out the whole de-bacle later on, I happen to know that, at first, the head of the de-partment was fairly balanced in his comments. The boss talked about what he thought of the underachieving team, and he asked for suggestions for change. But the team leader insisted that it wasn't his fault and that he didn't have any responsibility for the team's poor behavior, and soon the boss was very irritated.

It ended with his giving the team leader a harsh telling-off and forcefully questioning his competence. The "conversation" could be heard out in the corridor. He gave the team leader an earful, because the man refused to confront the problems apparent with his team.

The team leader's reaction was easy to predict. He deflated like a popped balloon. He got up from his chair, convinced that he would have to quit the company in shame. With his hand on the door handle, on his way out into the office to meet disapproving looks of his colleagues, he heard his formerly irate boss ask, "By the way, have you gotten lunch yet?"

This part of Red behavior is something that many people can't fathom. But it's precisely because the Reds distinguish between a situation and a person. Sure, the boss was angry with the team leader who refused to listen to the objective reality of the situation, and so he told him off. But he didn't detest the team leader and probably didn't even dislike him. He was dissatisfied with how the man behaved, and so he yelled. Then he noticed it was lunchtime and thought it would be nice to have a bit of company.

Hit the Gas! Why Are You Moving So Slowly?

Things get done at a hell of a speed. Reds work quickly. Sometimes they miss the details, but they keep up a furious pace in everything they do. And they have a lot of things going on at the same time. The feeling of urgency is also a typical Red trait. Even when there isn't really any need to rush, they're in a hurry. They like to get a lot done, and they're not happy sitting still.

A colleague and good friend of mine is a perfect example. He doesn't waste any time during a workday. If he has to wait for a taxi, he will check his email. If he's stuck in a traffic jam, he'll make a couple of phone calls. When he gets an email, he typically answers straightaway, because then it's done. The task of having to go back and check which email he has read and not answered just takes too much time. Waiting at airports, the same thing. Hotel rooms are basically designed for working. You can always squeeze in a little email, type up a clean copy of the meeting minutes, or prepare a presentation.

There are other colors beside Reds who demonstrate this same kind of efficiency. But they often do it in order to free up time later. They work a couple extra hours during an ordinary week and then go home at lunchtime on Friday. A Red doesn't do that. They don't go home just because they've finished. Instead, they take the opportunity to start on something new.

My favorite example is when my colleague was writing emails, participating in a video call, and listening to my presentation all at the same time. Even when the conversation on the video call became intense—in a language other than his native one—he didn't miss a single word of what I had to say. His analysis of the presentation was perfect. Multitasking is another strength for Reds. They can do numerous things simultaneously and process enormous amounts of information in a very short time. The trick is that they don't home in on the details; rather, they focus on the main features. They have an effective bird's-eye view, and they quickly see patterns in large amounts of information.

They care about the overall picture. Because the Reds don't like detail in the slightest. Urrgh!

What Does a Red Contribute to the Team?

The Red person makes sure that there is plenty of speed and action. Because they like to be on the move, they inspire others. Unless, of course, the Red is a total lone wolf—that happens, too. But the Red generates ideas, gives their opinion of the ideas of others, and ensures that decisions are made. While other colors find it hard to get to the heart of the matter, the Red will stand up during the meeting and say, "Okay, this is how we'll do it!" Then they'll go off and get it done. They'll probably create some sort of system for how the project should be completed. Although the Blue is primarily the one who creates detailed plans, the Red also likes to have a structure for how this and that should be done.

Later on, I'll describe the Red's main weaknesses and what an evil-minded person can do to get at the Red. Because, however tough they might seem, they do have their shortcomings. And the person who knows about these can easily make use of them for the purpose of manipulation.

Some Things You Need to Keep an Eye On

My opinion is that Red is the easiest color to deal with. Nevertheless, I meet lots of people in my work who think that Red behavior presents constant challenges. In fact, the problem is simple. The trick is not to take their behavior personally when you are on the receiving end of their somewhat brusque and clumsy style. If you can understand that their behavior is not directed specifically at you, then you'll manage just fine.

A simple way of dealing with the Reds at work is to always be well prepared. Make sure you have all the documentation and all the facts with you, make sure that you know what you want from the meeting and that you can answer questions if they come up. The Red might have questions or they might not. The clearer you express yourself, the fewer questions you'll encounter. But if the Red senses any uncertainty on your part, they'll definitely have questions. And they will be unrelenting. If the Red feels that you're being vague about certain facts, then they'll put the pressure on. So make sure you know what you're talking about.

And if it's a really important presentation, it's a good idea to practice exactly what you will say. Regardless of whether you are going to discuss your salary, apply for a new job, sell your services to a potential client, or present your project to your boss, practice your most important arguments. Reds like to challenge. If you have said that option B is superior (and say that only if you really believe it), don't change your mind if they challenge you. They may just be testing whether you really stand behind what you say. If you back down and say, "Sure, option C might work, too," then you've already lost. Now you look indecisive, and that won't help you in the slightest.

Imagine that you go to a cardiac specialist who says that the reason you feel so poorly is that you need a triple bypass operation. If you replied to this pronouncement by asking, "Wouldn't an ordinary double bypass be sufficient?" and the doctor answers, "Well, that might work; let's try it," would you let him operate on you after that? No, I thought not. And the Red wouldn't, either. They want to be sure that you really know what you're talking about.

When you meet Red people it's important that you focus on looking forward instead of talking about background. It's better to discuss the results you can achieve than the reasoning behind them. Describe—briefly—what you think option B can contribute and what targets you will reach with that particular solution. If the conversation does come around to the basis of your projections, go briefly through the background. That can be interesting, and Reds don't make baseless decisions every time, but they do prefer to talk about aims and results. Focus on that.

For God's Sake, Don't Do This!

Never waste a Red person's valuable time. That's what happens if you are poorly prepared: You'll give the impression of being disorganized. Make sure you have the right documents on your computer and don't sit there searching for the right information while the Red has to wait. If you waste twelve seconds of their life, then you've failed completely. They will drum their fingers on the tabletop faster than you can say "no deal here." If you are really unlucky, they'll pull out their cell phone and you'll have lost them.

If the discussion leads to your needing to get more information or documentation, then do it, if possible, in complete silence. The Red won't want to listen to your apologetic mumbling or nonsense about extenuating circumstances. They can wait in silence if *you* can manage it. Show that you're efficient. Get hold of the answer and give it to them.

Generally speaking, unimportant chitchat is a bad idea with Red people, even with those you know well. If the Red is a good friend and you're at a backyard barbecue, then it's okay to prattle on about where you may or may not go on vacation. But if you're sitting in your office, not even the normally easygoing Chris will want to know a bunch of irrelevant facts or gossip that you happened to have heard. Chris will want to know what the project consists of, whether you are going to earn any money, and how he'll profit from it. Don't start babbling about things that aren't on the agenda. And do everything quickly. You won't achieve that by talking faster but by using fewer words.

Then there's the question of being open and personal. Sure, I've been in positions where it's important to build a relationship with the client. But with Red people you need to think this through very carefully. They're not there to be your new tennis buddy; they're there to do business, and you had better remember that. Where the Red's wife studied psychology or his son plays football has nothing to do with you.

You might be thinking, *But I've been very personal with Red people that I hardly know. I've told them about my vacation in Vietnam, and they've told me about their trip to Bali.*

Sure. Red people might be impatient, but they're not stupid. They realize that they need to play along. Most of them are aware of the

fact that they can't just tell everyone to get lost, and that the majority of the population appreciates small talk. But remember this: They
would rather avoid it. If you help them save time by simply skipping
all the unnecessary blabber, then you'll make better business deals.
You'll gain their confidence and be seen as an ambitious and efficient
businessperson, colleague, coworker, or boss.

Finally, I want to remind you not to take the Red's direct manner
personally. The Red says what they think, and they rarely have nasty
intentions when they do so. They can demolish your extremely well-
prepared proposal in three sentences, and that's going to hurt. But it
isn't about you. You're not important in their eyes, not in that way.
The same thing applies in the opposite direction: If they applaud and
go along with your proposal, it doesn't imply that you will suddenly
be the best of buddies. It simply means that they liked your proposal.
The feedback on concrete issues will always be honest.

And when it comes to feedback: If you ask them what they think
about your new electric-pink shirt . . . well, you have only yourself
to blame.

Yellow (Influential) Behavior

The Joker, or Chatty Charlie

The smile. Nobody smiles more than the Yellows. There is always
something to smile at. And why not? Life is great, don't you think?
You can also recognize a Yellow person from their openness and
their quick manner of speaking. They talk freely about anything and
everything. And they talk a lot. If you want to quickly identify a
Yellow person, look for someone who is standing in the middle of a
group of people and talking a lot. And many of their sentences start
with the revealing word "I."

Heartiness. They will make you feel good and feel seen. A firm
handshake, but not too firm. They don't have the same need to domi-

nate that Red people have, but they will often put their free hand on your arm to show just how wonderful it is to meet *YOU*. And it works. People glow in the company of the Yellow.

After a while, however, you may notice that even though the Yellow asks you questions all the time, they don't seem to actually listen to your answer. They are not very good listeners. They're mainly talkers and people who can create a warm atmosphere. Soon we secretly start wondering whether they would be just as happy without us.

Probably not. The Yellow is a decidedly social being. They want people around them. If they're forced into a lonely office without company, they will probably wither away and die. They will always be found where there are people. They have a rich social life, know loads of people, and have a contact list on their cell phone that is longer than you can imagine. And you don't have to talk with them long before they ask what your Instagram handle is. You're friends now! Yes!

Beyond the Laughter and Smiles

The Yellow will always be more creative than the rest of us. This doesn't mean that they're the only ones who come up with ideas, but they do have a rare ability to turn a thought upside down and make you wonder how they came up with it. Then they shrug their shoulders and smile. Again. If you think it was an idea worth considering, then you should write it down, because the Yellow probably won't. Documentation is not their strongest suit. Typically, they just scribble something on a Post-it. We can do the details later. Or never.

Not so very long ago, I met a tech entrepreneur who bubbled over with creativity. She talked nonstop, elaborating about her big plans, opportunities she had identified, and projects she was in the midst of launching. And, sure, she was doing a lot. There was no doubt about that. But if she had actually done even half of what she talked about, she would have achieved world domination by now. Instead, her business was just treading water and getting by. The reason, in my opinion, was that she surrounded herself with people who were exactly like her. There were about twenty people working for her, and all of them were just as happy and bright and positive and ready to get down to work. But there was virtually no structure. They were juggling lots of balls at the same time, but far too many of these balls simply dropped like windfalls off an apple tree, landing on someone's head on the way down.

The workplace itself was a veritable disaster area. The entire office was chockablock with clutter, and the meeting room looked like a war zone. The staff didn't think it mattered, since they saw it as a creative environment. That's all very well, but mess and disorganization are not the same thing as creativity. This is where things can come to a halt for Yellows. They find it hard to keep track of the small things, which often prevents them from looking after the bigger ones. Clients were not terribly impressed when they came to a fancy address and stepped right into what looked like a hurricane.

This entrepreneur's uncompleted projects were endless, which provides an important insight into Yellow behavior. They are superb at starting things, but they don't have the ability to follow through. For that, you need a different behavior type.

The Whole World Is One Big Audience

As I've already mentioned, Yellows are extremely open. You can take it for granted that you will be updated on their family and see photos of the children and the dog and their best friend. A Yellow person's office will be filled to the brim with personal things that can tell you a lot about them.

At one consulting firm where I worked, we had something called a "clean-desk policy," inaugurated by our Red-Yellow CEO. In theory, it meant that you were obliged to put away all your things when you left your desk. There were more employees than there were desks because we were expected to be out of the office consulting with clients (consultants are often more profitable out at a client's rather than sitting in their own office). Thus, the policy only worked if the number of desks on a given day matched the number of employees needing one. If it got a bit cramped in the office, the CEO simply answered, "You're right there's a problem, but not the one you think. Why are you even here?"

For me, this wasn't a problem. Although I have some Yellow in my profile, I have never had much paraphernalia on my desk. Besides, I like orderliness and things in their place, which means that I clean up regularly. That might be because I also have quite a lot of Blue in my profile and I have an aesthetic driver, which means that I feel better when things are nice and tidy around me.

But the Yellow consultants believed that the CEO had made a big mistake with his clean-desk policy. They couldn't see the point of cleaning up after themselves. It got messy all over again anyway! And the rule about not putting personal things on your desk? Why not? They had pictures of the kids and sports car, and where were they supposed to put them? Yellow people don't notice when things begin to get messy. They have no desire to have things in the same place. It was quite an ordeal to get the policy up and running, I can promise you that.

On the other hand, there were few people who could clinch as many good business deals as the Yellow consultants. They were always buzzing around, and the telephones were constantly in use. If anybody could open doors and convince clients of the most ludicrous solutions, it was the Yellows. They could just talk right over the client's decision-makers with their gift of gab. They are superb communicators and find it easy and natural to use the right words. Everything a Yellow person says sounds great. When you hear a description of the product or the plan, you want to shout, "Yes! Give it to me!"

With the right support, nothing will get in the way of a Yellow. They will inspire the masses to great deeds by standing on a chair and reeling off a spontaneous speech as easily as you might write a text message to your mother. Envious? I can see why. For many people, speaking in public is one of the worst things. This doesn't apply to Yellow people. They happily speak in public for as long as you'll let them; the challenge is getting them off the podium.

What Does a Yellow Contribute to the Team?

The Yellow coworker motivates and inspires their colleagues by encouraging and praising them. They hand out compliments, which most people appreciate. Even though they're brilliant communicators, they'll often let others express themselves. They ask for opinions and ideas and create a warm atmosphere for the team. And don't forget their positive attitude. When everything is a mess and some of your colleagues are ready to pack up their desks, the Yellow will come along and give the group new courage. The Yellow's inspiring attitude will rub off on everything and everyone.

They do have their weaknesses, however, and we'll get to those. Just as it is with Reds, it's simple to take advantage of a Yellow's weaknesses—as long as you know how. Later on, I'll have an example of how this can happen, and if you're Yellow, then you ought to read very carefully to protect yourself from manipulation.

It's a good idea to keep things in order if you want to handle a Yellow behavior.

Smile! And Follow the Advice Below!

People often comment that Yellows are *so nice. What a great guy!* And they are. Yellows are nice, funny, entertaining, humorous, and easygoing. But Yellows will also want *you* to be fun and creative as well. They want to be inspired in turn and to surround themselves with people who are just like themselves. My biggest advice when it comes to meeting a Yellow person is just this: Smile!

I don't think I'll shock you when I say that most people appreciate a smile more than a grumpy attitude, but smiling is especially important for your future relationship with a Yellow. Smiling shows a Yellow that you're happy and naturally positive—exactly the type of person that they want to be with.

But if you're a bit morose and sulky, they'll feel uncomfortable. They understand that there is bad news in the world, but they don't want to hear it. They want ice cream and balloons all the time, and the best thing you can do is make sure that you offer them precisely that. Be happy and smile, even when you tell them that the cat fell off the roof or that their major deal was a total flop. You can deal with damage control later.

Build relationships. Dare to share who you are. Give something of yourself. Don't be afraid to say what you think about running or cars or cozy evenings at home. The Yellow will like you better and think you are personable. They are (almost too) open with themselves and their lives. You'll soon be best mates if you give something back.

The same applies to that social small talk that Reds are allergic to. The Yellows expect it. They want to talk about the weather, the game last night, and whether Prague will be the next hot travel destination for trendsetters. But remember that politics isn't a good subject since it probably involves some problems or bad news. Yellows want the conversation to be positive and easygoing. They don't want to hear a word about the leader of the free world or the state of Congress.

How to Make a Yellow an Enemy for Life

There are some things that Yellow people are very sensitive to. They don't like what they consider to be coldness or lack of feeling. Not smiling is a good example. If you are very serious, as many Blue people are, then you might have a problem. They will think of you as a downer, and Yellows don't appreciate that. If you don't laugh at the right time, they will feel uncomfortable and start to think you dislike them.

It can be just as bad to push a Yellow person into a very detail-oriented discussion with lots of facts and figures. Yellows find details to be a real pain. What on earth does it matter whether it is 33.67 or 34 degrees outside? The Yellow doesn't care if they show up fifteen minutes or eighteen minutes late. What's all the fuss? They're here *now*!

Sometimes this can be expressed in rather amusing ways. A Yellow person might come to you and declare that you simply MUST try this new downtown restaurant. The food there is FANTASTIC! When you (smiling, of course) ask where the restaurant actually is, they can't really remember. The name of the restaurant is also shrouded in mystery. And if you asked what they actually ate, there's no guarantee they'd remember that either. But they do know that you ought to go there and order the same dish, because it is unbelievable. Now the rest is up to you.

Make sure that your Yellow colleague, friend, or partner gets enough space in the conversation. They are, admittedly, good at helping themselves to the spotlight, but if you happen to be a more dominant person (read: Red), then you might be tempted to just hold up a hand and shush them. I don't recommend that. You will get an offended look, and they won't listen to what you have to say. In fact, nobody likes being told to keep quiet, although many of you Reds will probably keep telling people anyway.

If you have criticism to share with a Yellow, choose your moment with care. If you are a boss and have a Yellow coworker who has messed things up, remember: Do not give them negative feedback publicly. This is extremely important with Yellow people in particular. Negative criticism hurts the Yellow's rather big ego, and you might end up with a new enemy.

Green (Stable) Behavior

The King of Coziness, or Comfortable Connie

The clearest sign that you're dealing with a Green person is that they're not in your way. They are compliant and discreet. They don't want to be in the middle of anything and would rather have somebody else make the decisions. They will happily hand responsibility over to you or anyone else nearby. There is a lot of *Oh, I couldn't . . .* with a Green person. It's unusual for Green people to challenge anyone in a discussion. They might not always agree, but they don't openly state their opinions. However, when they're with their best friend later on, they'll definitely say what they really think of your new, badly thought-through proposal. The biggest mistake you can make with a Green person is to assume that they don't have any opinion at all. They do. They just don't share it.

Since they strive for stability and prefer to avoid change, they'll leave things as they are. *It's fine the way it is. You know what you have, but you never know what you'll get* are typical Green comments. And that's true. Why change something just for the sake of change? They see most change, especially rapid change, with deep suspicion. Amusingly, Green people often deny this. *Of course I like change,* they say. Right up until you propose something new.

The Green colleague is often extremely caring. They will refill the coffee machine, make that extra trip to the post office, ask how you're feeling and whether your back pain is still flaring up. They'll remember your migraine from so long ago that you hardly remember it yourself.

They work best on a team. Being by themselves is not optimal for a Green person, despite being introverted. They don't feel the need to talk all the time. For them, it's enough to just be in the same room as their coworkers. And at home, quality time can mean sitting in front of the TV together.

They're Everywhere

Working with a Green person is fairly easy to do. Because they'll let you do what you want, you won't need to adapt to them much. They don't demand anything for themselves, which makes it easy for people around them. This tendency can be easily abused by certain individuals, but more about that later.

I remember one particularly good example from an insurance company where I was working on a special project. This team consisted of about fifty people, and the boss was Yellow–Blue. He had ideas and was often inspired to think up new things, and his team wanted to be loyal and follow along. Even if they didn't like the changes, they appreciated their boss and listened to him. But since he also had a lot of Blue in him, sometimes this meant he'd pull the emergency brake and bring things to a quick halt. While the Yellow part of his behavior pushed for new ideas and projects, the Blue side insisted that the idea had to be analyzed thoroughly.

The effect was a little odd. Lots of people thought that everything functioned well but went along with changes anyway because they didn't want to oppose the boss. They went through the work of getting themselves excited about a new idea, but just as they started adjusting to the new system, the boss came back and said that his groundbreaking idea probably wouldn't work out after all. This resulted in a state of continual mental limbo. *Will we* or *won't we* change the routines, the furniture, our lunch hour, the organization? Nobody knew. And that isn't good for anybody. But it's particularly unfortunate if you have a group of Green people, because they want to know. They need to be informed about what is going on. Too much vagueness creates stress.

This went on year in and year out in large part because Green people are, in general, extremely loyal. They wanted to be faithful to the boss and do their best for the company. Even if it means making themselves miserable, Green people want everyone to be happy.

Loyalty is an important quality for Greens. They are loyal to those closest to them. Their family, their neighborhood, the people who drive the same make of car as them, their football or bowling league. At work, it's about their immediate work team. They are most loyal to the people they know best. This can lead to problems, though. If the organization is very large, they won't necessarily feel much loyalty toward top management or to the vision the company is trying to create. They focus more on what is happening around their own desk. And if their coworkers say they are discontent, then the Greens will think the same.

This is a rather complicated psychology, but the basic rule is that Greens agree with the people they have confidence in. If you know who these people are, you can work out what they are most likely to think.

The Best Friend in the Entire World

I've already mentioned it, but the Green is friendliness incarnate. They hold open the door for you; they let the children eat ice cream even though it's a Tuesday and dinner is going to be ready in thirty minutes; they are the person you ask to keep an eye on your dog while you're in the supermarket for ten minutes. If you lose your wallet and a Green finds it, the wallet will be returned and you will be asked to make sure nothing is missing. It would be absurd of me to claim that Green people can't steal anything, because it isn't as simple as that. But they are basically honest and don't want to harm anybody. That is an important driving force for them. They want to be able to rely on others, and they want others to be able to rely on them.

Calmness is another positive attribute that many Greens have. They're not the type to get stressed. That doesn't mean that they're always as cool as a cucumber, but they have a basic stability that is very useful when things start getting heated. If you have a gang of

Yellow individuals in high spirits running around and not getting much done, send a couple of Green people into the group. They will cool down the worst disasters and make sure order is restored.

In a work team, you always know where the Green is. They're exactly where you left them. Management can count on them not to think up harebrained schemes or go off the rails. And should they have a crazy idea, they won't act on it without hammering out the details. (To be perfectly honest, even once the boss has approved such an idea, nothing much might happen.)

Yellow and Red people have a much shorter path between idea and action. A Red person is up out of their chair before they even know what needs to be done, and the Yellow will start recruiting as many adherents as they can and set everything in motion.

The Greens don't do that. If they think the instructions were unclear or that the management's enthusiasm is weak, nothing will happen. The advantages of a Green workforce are obvious. The management can be sure that they'll avoid any unpleasant surprises. The Green team will continue to work toward the same goals as before. No new orders will be necessary, and following up isn't terribly important. They'll stick to the original plan and simply get on with the job.

What Does a Green Contribute to the Team?

Greens obviously make great team players! They often have new insights due to their calmness. Since they are good at asking others for their opinions and then listening properly to the answers—and remembering them—they help create a good team dynamic. Everyone has a say and more ideas get shared. Very few people feel threatened by Green behavior.

I have already touched on the Greens' weaknesses: On the whole, they are a little too easy to exploit because they are so friendly and accommodating. Later on, we'll have a look at how that happens.

Since your Green friend is slightly introverted, remember the following. Especially this: Go easy. That's the best advice I can give you. When you think you've got a tip-top idea that everyone is going to love, remind yourself that the Green is already satisfied with the status quo. The best path to their approval is to sit down with a cup of coffee and start asking how they feel. A few slightly personal questions about what they're up to will show that you are interested in them as people. Then you can carefully broach the subject you really want to discuss.

I realize that you can't devote five minutes of softening up to the beginning of every conversation, but if you have a bigger issue to raise with a Green person, it's a good idea to begin slowly. Show interest in order to ensure they are mentally present. But, like I said, go easy. Don't expect any applause for your idea. Their reaction might well be . . . nothing special.

By all means, ask for the Green's opinion. They have one, but they won't divulge it just like that. Weird? Not at all, not if you are Green. They want to know what you think first so that they can adapt the answer to you. The problem here is obvious: you want to know what they genuinely think, not hear your opinion repeated back. But since they want to please you, you'll have to try something else. Ask lots of questions. Ask for suggestions. Ask them what this or that idea would mean for the team. Not for the Green personally, but for the group, the team, the company. Remember that for a Green, the group has priority over the individual.

It's important to realize you are not necessarily going to get any straight answers from them. Green people rarely give straight answers; instead, they'll tiptoe around for a while. Sometimes this is going to really irritate you, but if you know the key to dealing with Greens, you'll be fine.

The key is to arm yourself with a hefty dose of patience. You'll need to make use of the step-by-step method. It's simple. Convey your message in small portions. Divide it up—especially if you suspect that what you have to say might be controversial—into several different meetings and conversations. If you need to delegate a project, you might need to discuss it a little bit at a time on Monday, Wednesday, and Friday.

The advantage to this method is that the Green will have time to digest what you've said, process it on their own, and formulate their own questions, making it easier for you to get the approval you need. Once all the corners of the new thing have been investigated, they'll swallow the bait and become loyal to the new project or whatever it is you are dealing with.

It wouldn't surprise me if some of you who are reading this think, *Fine, but do you really think that I've got time for that?* But it doesn't make any difference. This is how you reach the Green.

Remember this: Go easy.

Do This If You Really Want to Stress Out a Green

After what I've said above, it's pretty obvious what is going to work badly with a Green. Get a Green all hot and bothered or stress them out by demanding quick answers or rapid decisions, and every-thing will become a mess and you won't get what you want. Red people have the hardest time with Greens. Red behavior is task-oriented and quick; Green behavior is relationship-oriented and de-liberate. Reds will often put their foot in it by looking a Green person in the eye and telling them that "this is what we're doing!" Often in all-capital letters. Dominant behavior is not going to work. You're talking to a person who always gives priority to the group, and you're doing so in a way that clearly shows that you give priority to your-self. These are completely different worlds.

It's important to proceed with caution. If you barge in and start ranting about a to-do list right off the bat, your Green colleague will think you're a pain. They'll nod and smile since they want to be rid of you, but when you've left, they will put your piece of paper at the bottom of the pile. It isn't a question of not understanding; they know perfectly well that what you asked them to do is a priority. But since you behaved like a jerk, they'll punish you by doing . . . nothing.

Another thing to keep in mind is how to delegate. Greens are not normally competitive people (though there are exceptions; there always are). So if your targets or goals are far too ambitious, this won't have any direct effect on their behavior. Whereas a Red would be prepared to break their neck to stick to the budget, the Green will simply sit on the sofa with their cup of coffee, convinced that the target is so unrealistic that it isn't even worth trying. They're not results-driven. Instead, they're more like that nurse who volunteers to work an extra night shift at the hospital because the ER is flooded with patients and a coworker has the flu. That's a significant achievement, but it's done quietly and without fanfare.

Last but not least: If you can avoid arguments, that would be ideal. Greens are afraid of conflict. They don't like it at all when things get tense. If you contradict a Green person with the slightest note of frustration in your voice, they can interpret this as a potential conflict, and you risk blocking all communication between you. Just because you wanted to make it clear that you don't think the office is too cold can be enough to put the Green in a sulk. Did you have to be so mean? I'm not suggesting that you have to pretend you need another sweater, just that you should tread softly when you reply to a Green.

Blue (Compliant) Behavior

The Controller, or Analytical Alan

Meeting a Blue person might not be an immediately fantastic experience. The first thing you'll notice is an extremely neutral face—not negative, but neutral. They have their facial muscles under control and they're not going to fire off a movie-star smile at you just because that is what you do. They smile when there is something to smile at. Full stop. Their body language is balanced. The Blue will never be one of those people who resorts to big gestures. Even their handshake is hard to comment on. They won't shake your hand without having a good reason to do so. And there rarely is a reason.

Their speech is calm and often well formulated. Many Blue people talk with such a neutral voice that listeners find it hard to stay focused on their words. This is because Blues often believe that content is more important than presentation. Facts are facts.

You'll be able to recognize a Blue person from their evident calmness. They don't let themselves become upset over every little thing. If you were to explode a bomb near them, they would come, look at the rubble, and wonder how it was constructed. If they come home to a surprise party where their entire senior class has secretly gathered together, they would probably smile when the lights were turned on (although that's not guaranteed), but their comment would be something like "that was nice." That's how they are; they don't overdo things, oh no.

A Few Points to Note

I once got a question from a manager who was participating in a training program that included the use of the DISC analytical tool. He wondered how you could analyze someone who didn't do anything. When I asked him what he meant, he told me about a coworker who hardly moved at all. This person sat perfectly still in their office chair in front of the computer all day long. He didn't take part in the usual workplace conversations, and he definitely didn't smile unnecessarily. His face was carved in stone, and this manager suspected there was something wrong with him.

I asked him whether this person was extremely detail-oriented, and he confirmed that was true. Evidently the coworker was an Excel wizard and brilliant with numbers in general. Nobody could ever find fault with him when it came to dealing with data of various kinds. He could reel off long sections from different manuals and handbooks, and he only disrupted his work if someone interrupted his routine.

"Well," I said, "there's actually quite a lot to analyze here." To which the manager replied, "Yes, but he just sits there!" Which led me to ask him. "And works?" There you have it. The coworker was Blue through and through. So he sat at his desk and did exactly what he was meant to do instead of hovering around the office and wasting time.

This is one of the advantages of Blue behavior. Although Blue people might not attract a crowd of admirers or tell funny jokes or inspire those around them, they get on with their job. They figure out what a task entails, plan their work, and carry it out. Simple, right? That's what you need to get the job done. Blues are extremely task-oriented while at the same time being exceptionally introverted. This is the quietest profile of all. They only talk when they have something important to say.

Don't expect any feedback or praise from a Blue unless you ask for it. Your Blue colleague or partner or friend is not going to spontaneously stop when they have seen what you've done and say, "Wow, that turned out really well!" If you were to ask them what they think, they'd probably answer you right away, and you would also be given some unsolicited advice on how you could have done everything much, much better.

Blues have an extremely critical eye. They see every shortcoming at a glance, and they tend to harp on what has gone wrong. They don't see the big picture, but get stuck on the details. Even if you have completely renovated your kitchen, your Blue neighbor will point out that one cupboard door is a bit crooked. Just like Reds, Blues are going to say what they think—without using a euphemism or wrapping their words in a pretty package. You'll simply have to accept that.

Everything in Order, Just as It Should Be

I've already said that the Blue is task-oriented—that is, has a matter-of-fact manner. They'll normally stick to the subject and not stray from the agenda. They do one job at a time. Nothing they do seems to involve making much of a fuss, a simple and unpretentious approach that is sometimes liberating. The Blue person rarely sends emails bragging about their latest successes. Instead, they hand in a sales report to the CEO with the biggest business deal of the year neatly noted on line twelve.

When the CEO rushes into the seller's office and gushes over the fantastic deal, the Blue will just look at their boss—with that same neutral expression—and explain that they only did their job. I wouldn't go so far as to say that Blue people don't need positive feedback or praise, but they don't put much emphasis on it. When I have praised the incredible contributions made by Blue sellers, I've always been met with a simple "thank you." It's not that Blues find public praise uncomfortable—it's the Green person who dreads it—but they don't seek it. They can go up onto a stage to be feted and given flowers but then step down again and go right back to their desk. It's not quite five o'clock yet.

And that's another trait to look for. Blue people are often punctual. Yes, there are exceptions—I know a number of Blue people who can't seem to read the clock—but on the whole, you don't need to remind the Blue that we're going to be meeting at four o'clock. *You said that in January, why are you bringing it up again?*

This is noticeable even when it comes to office hours. I often hear comments like this: "George, over there, just watch; he's going to get up at exactly five o'clock and leave." Regardless of where he is with his work. And indeed, like clockwork, George goes home at five o'clock sharp. Why? Well, you have to stop working sometime, and why not at the generally accepted hour of five o'clock? And we can be certain that he will leave the office at exactly the same time every day. Why? Well, why not?

What Does the Blue Contribute to the Team?

This is actually an interesting question. Since the Blue person naturally digs rather deep to find all the facts and possible solutions to a problem, they will help the group get to the bottom of a problem. The Blue person always asks more questions than anyone else, which means that you aren't going to miss important information. Once you finally make a decision, if there's a Blue in the group you can be confident that every angle has been examined. And it's a good feeling to know that you can rely on somebody, isn't it?

Later in the book, I'll explain how the Blue person can find themselves in trouble when it comes to manipulative and deceptive behavior. But I can already give you a clue. It's fairly difficult to fool a Blue person. They're going to check up on what you say. And if you've bluffed, they will know. More about this later.

Ways to Avoid Damaging Your Relationship with a Blue
USE FACTS AND BEHAVE CORRECTLY

What do we do with this reticent individual who is as cool as a cucumber? The simplest way of handling a Blue person is probably to stick to the subject. Just like the Reds, they come to the office to work. So make sure that you do the same and you'll get the best from them. It might sound a bit self-righteous when I point this out. Perhaps you're thinking that of course you work when you're at your office. That's what you're getting paid for, so of course you do. But you also know that some of your time is spent on other things—on surfing the internet, going on errands, chatting nonsense by the coffee machine. We all do this to varying degrees.

Except your Blue coworkers. They sit at their desk and get on with the job. If you want to gain their confidence, make sure you gain a reputation as someone who does their work. If you're going to work together, make sure you are really, really well prepared for the task. You can't turn up at a meeting without being thoroughly familiar with the paperwork or having badly presented material. The Blue will immediately judge you if you don't know exactly what you're doing. They might not say it out loud, as the Red would do, but they'll definitely notice that you can't find the right document.

Similarly, you should check all your facts. Say that you're going to present something to a Blue client. A proposal or a new project or whatever. Do some research and find out about the background. As you stand in front of them and wave your arms around, the Blue person will be wondering: How do you know this? Where is this data from? You need to explain exactly how you have reached your conclusion and why this particular proposal is best. Even if you think that you went through the background at your previous meeting, you ought to refer back and make sure the client sees what you see. They might have done some research of their own in the meanwhile. If you don't understand their perspective, check where they're standing, you will miss the target.

Don't expect any excitement. Even if your presentation was absolutely perfect and the Blue person gets exactly what they asked for, be aware that they won't feel the need to give you feedback. Either they will accept what you say or they won't. If you are lucky, they'll say (still with that stone face that makes you feel panicky) that it "sounds fine." That's it.

Do you want the conversation to flow smoothly? Then talk about details, facts, and how you are going to pay special attention to the finer points when you carry it out in the proposal. Talk about planning, about structure, and about keeping everything in order. You'll do brilliantly.

AVOID DEVIANT AND OTHER UNAPPRECIATED BEHAVIOR

Just like the Green person, the Blue does not like it when you put them under pressure. They want to take their time. There is, however, an important difference: While the Green will feel stressed by the idea of making a decision, the Blue person is interested in the process itself. If you try to force the pace, it won't go well. You have to let things take the time they take. If you push too hard, you'll just get a short "no thank you." Or they'll stop answering the phone. That has happened to me several times.

When you work with Blue people, you should avoid all carelessness. But remember this: If you are not a Blue, you're going to think you are fully in control of everything. In the Blue's world, however, you might not be so impressive—they're going to read every word you have written about a report or a project. But they'll also note every little spelling mistake, every crooked column, or whether the fonts are different in the Excel spreadsheets. Yet again, they might not say anything about it. But they'll observe it and add it to the list of observations they have made of you. You can be sure it will factor into their understanding of who you are and whether you are a reliable person.

When it comes to factual information, it's okay to answer a direct question by saying that you don't know and would like to get back to them. Just making something up to get off the hook won't work.

On one occasion, a year or so ago, I had put together a proposal for a sales program for about 180 participants. It concerned a three-day course and there was lots of documentation, online learning, and other things that went along with it. Well aware of the fact that the decision-maker was fairly Blue (and had a bit of Red), I had been extremely detailed in my presentation. Most of our meeting dealt with figures, but there was one thing I'd missed. I hadn't worked out the price per person. That wasn't exactly a serious error, but when the question cropped up, I made the mistake of trying to work it out on the spot. The decision-maker nodded silently, noted the figure, and we moved on. However, I had forgotten part of the fixed costs for the conference center, which meant that the figure I had given him was incorrect. The client was not slow to point this out at our next meeting. He had, of course, checked the figures. I don't really think he doubted me before he checked the math, but as a Blue you always double-check. It's a natural behavior, but that time it created some problems for me. I still work with this client, but it would have been a lot better if I had said I would get back to him with the correct figure.

Quality, my friend, is everything. Absolutely everything.

The DISC Model

Here are a few things to know about the DISC model:

- Not everything in an individual's behavior can be explained by the DISC model.
- There are other models that explain behavior, but I use this as the basis because it is simple to digest and to teach. There are more parts of the puzzle than the colors to map various behavior patterns.
- The DISC model is based on thorough studies and is used throughout the world. It has been translated into more than fifty different languages.
- Historically, there are similar views in different cultures—for example, the four humors described by Hippocrates, who lived in Greece about 2,500 years ago.
- About 80 percent of all people have a combination of two colors that dominate their behavior. Approximately 5 percent have only one color that dominates behavior. The others are dominated by three colors.

- Entirely Green behavior, or Green in combinations with one other color, is the most common. The least common is entirely Red behavior, or Red behavior in combination with one other color.
- There may be differences between the sexes, but I do not deal with the gender perspective in this book.
- The DISC model does not work for analyzing people with ADHD, Asperger's, borderline personality disorder, or other disorders.
- There are always exceptions to what I claim in this book. People are complex—even Red people can be humble, and Yellows can listen attentively. There are Green people who deal with conflict because they have learned what to do, and many Blues understand when it's time to stop fact-checking.
- Everything described above is about self-awareness. Problems in communications arise when people lack self-awareness.
- My own colors are Red and Blue and a bit of Yellow. No Green to speak of. Sorry.

5

Manipulation Is Everywhere

People generally cannot believe themselves so easily manipulated and controllable. This is precisely why they are so easy to manipulate and control.

—Wilson Bryan Key

What Is Manipulation? And Is It Always Negative?

Now it's time to take things seriously. The answer to the second question in the heading is this: not necessarily. All relationships contain some sort of influence or persuasion. And that's natural, isn't it? The man who negotiates with his wife so that he can go on a fishing trip. Or the wife who feigns a headache when he wants to visit his brother and have a barbecue. Fairly innocent activities that can be irritating but that we know occur all the time. Manipulation is part of the social game, and we come across it every day.

There is a lot of positive influence in the world, too: Your doctor who tries to get you to change your diet because she's worried about your health. Teachers who try to persuade our children to take school seriously. Parents who encourage the same children to do their homework and get good grades on exams by promising them an allowance if they get high grades. Raising children is basically eighteen years of exercising influence. But at least it's for a good purpose. That type of influence involves respect for the person you are trying to influence. My motives are good. I want the best for him or her.

If we look in the thesaurus, we'll find the following suggestions under "manipulate": "control, influence, use to one's advantage, exploit." Manipulation means to consciously attempt to change things out of self-interest. The word in itself might not have any real emotional charge, but for most people it has a negative sense when describing psychological manipulation. (Try presenting your new fiancée like this: "Lisa is an absolute dear, she's pretty, and she makes me laugh. And she is a brilliant manipulator." No.)

A manipulator uses deceptive methods to change something about someone—say, that person's opinion on a certain issue—without their realizing the real purpose. Which is inherently egoistic.

If I try to talk somebody into lending me money without having any intention of ever repaying the loan, that is a negative manipulation. The benefit to me is obvious: I get the money but don't have to pay it back. 1-0 to me.

If I console and encourage and praise somebody in order to make them feel better, that is what psychologists call positive manipulation. But there might also be benefits for me: When my wife is happy, she might make dinner, and I won't have to do it. I've chosen to call this phenomenon "influence" rather than manipulation.

Children who want something—another ice cream or to stay up an extra half hour—and who know that there is a high chance of hearing a straight no often flatter their parents or empty the dishwasher before they ask the question. The woman who suffers through her husband's favorite show so that he'll come with her to dinner with her parents over the weekend. The man who promises to finish fixing the deck if he can upgrade the sound system.

Let's be honest. At one time or another, most of us have been exploited. We've all come across somebody who makes sure they gain something at our expense. It might be something small. A colleague who always asks for help when he has an impending deadline but who never reciprocates the favor when you need a helping hand. Or a neighbor who always borrows something and never gives it back, knowing that you are too kind to make a fuss. Perhaps you, just like me, have opened your wallet far too many times because somebody has convinced you it's your responsibility. And sometimes it's easiest just to play along.

You've Done It to Somebody—Confess!

And now, since we're being honest, all of us have used others one way or another. From your own perspective, it often doesn't look like exerting influence. It could be me sending someone to do an errand I could easily do myself. But I don't feel like it, so I say I haven't got time. Or I have a drink a little too early in the morning while on vacation and say that it's good for my stomach. But in fact, I just fancied a drink. These are all examples of influence. And we influence each other as well. Just by writing this line of text—to get you to say to yourself, *Yes, that's just how it is!*—is a form of influence. I wanted to get you to agree with me.

However, most everyday social influence is relatively innocent and harmless. Very few of us would ever try to use our influence for something more serious, like trying to persuade a bank official to reveal the code to the bank vault.

Psychological manipulation is a type of social influence with the purpose of changing the behavior of others by using hidden or deceptive methods or by using mental or physical encroachment. It favors the manipulator at the expense of the manipulated and is thus an abuse of power, an exploitation of somebody's goodwill, and a type of deception. Psychopaths use classic psychological manipulation, but they do it so elegantly that we're not aware of it. They have to hide their behavior in order to ensure that we don't notice we're being manipulated.

An Example of Subtle Manipulation

A woman wants to have renovations done around the house—change the flooring, update the bathroom, and such. Her husband grumbles at first about how much work it will be, but finally agrees. He decides to do all the work himself. She asks him what he thinks it's going to cost, and after a bit of math he answers, about $7,500. She gives him the money from the account tied to her paycheck, since it's easier to access. He hasn't contributed anything to that account at all, but that doesn't bother him. The woman isn't concerned either, since this is her husband. Of course she trusts the person she has married. And, anyway, the renovations are for the house they share.

The materials start to arrive, and he gets to work on the renovation. But pretty soon the money is gone and he needs more to finish the work. Maybe he forgot to factor in the wallpaper or they wanted to upgrade to a nicer type of wood flooring. She wants everything to look beautiful, and she's the one who suggested the renovation in the first place. So she transfers even more money. And the renovation continues.

But hold on a moment. *Is this really psychological manipulation?* you might be wondering. It sounds more like . . . an ordinary home-renovation project.

On the surface, perhaps, but if we look closer, we see something strange. The man doesn't have any of the receipts for all the materials he has bought. A month after the project has been completed, bills start arriving from the building suppliers, all of them addressed to the woman. The invoices are for flooring, ceiling panels, wallpaper, and much more. The woman is confused—after all, she already gave him money for these costs. Why is she receiving bills for them now?

But the man reassures her. It just ended up costing a bit more than was estimated, and she did—as he likes to remind her—want the very best. Besides, the supplier made a mistake on the bill, but he promises to go there straightaway and sort it out. Which, of course, he never does.

So the woman pays. Again. Now she has paid for the renovation twice. Or perhaps four times. Who knows what the whole thing really *ought* to cost?

The psychopath, the man in this case, couldn't care less about the truth. He wanted to play poker on the internet and hid "the small sums" in the renovation. He might very well have used half or even all the money on nonsense. His manipulation succeeds because he knows his wife very, very well. He knows that she is uninterested in details, that she doesn't want to know what the screws cost. She has really no idea what a renovation like this should cost, and if she were to start asking questions, he can just raise his voice and act offended. *How can she doubt him?*

A perfect example of psychological manipulation in everyday life. Nobody is physically hurt. Nobody dies. But, nevertheless, the psychopath has conned his wife into paying large sums of money for things she never would have agreed to. Sadly, this example was taken from real life, and the man used the money to go on secret dates with other women.

Eternal Influence

We try to influence each other all the time. We argue and discuss, weigh advantages against disadvantages, and hope that our proposal wins. But as long as there is a good purpose and there is no hidden agenda, this is just influence, nothing else. If I change a person's opinion by lying and deceiving, that is an act of manipulation. If I try to force a person to do something they don't want to do, that is manipulation.

It's sometimes very difficult to say where the border is, but if there is an evil intention, a hidden motive, or a secret agenda—that is manipulation.

Most of us don't manipulate each other. We have our conscience to deal with. If I trick Leif into taking the blame for something I've done wrong at work, then I'll find it hard to look him in the eye in the future. Even just being in the same room as him would be a challenge. But if I don't have a conscience, if I never feel any remorse and if I don't care about him or his feelings one little bit, then I can do whatever I wish to poor Leif.

Why Do We Manipulate Each Other?

We want something from the other person, something that we can't get any other way. Or at least something we can't get in an easier or quicker way. There are loads of reasons, and sometimes it comes down to an individual's driving force, or motivational factors, if you like. There are lots of driving forces: love, sex, power, money, and others. In the workplace, there are primarily six driving forces:

- Theoretical Driving Force
- Practical–Economic Driving Force
- Aesthetic Driving Force
- Social Driving Force
- Individualistic Driving Force
- Traditional Driving Force

Let's take a brief look at each driving force. Reflect upon which driving force(s) tend to influence you.

Theoretical Driving Force

This force is motivated by a desire to learn and acquire more knowledge. Individuals influenced by this driving force are typically thoughtful and pensive. They don't normally judge things by their appearance but want to understand the underlying context. Since a person with strong theoretical driving force is usually critical, rational, and data driven, they are often thought of as intellectuals or academics. They are often interested in sorting and categorizing knowledge.

Practical-Economic Driving Force

The practical–economic driving force reveals itself through a strong interest in money and other purely practical things. For these people, the security and freedom that economic resources can provide are important—for themselves and their family. People with a strong practical–economic driving force are often very business-minded. They often see material resources and status objects as deeply important.

Aesthetic Driving Force

Those who have a strong aesthetic driving force are often interested in design and harmony. As a rule, they appreciate objects and experiences for their aesthetic qualities and form. People with a strong aesthetic driving force will notice and appreciate details that others fail to observe. This driving force doesn't necessarily mean that a person is artistically gifted, but they do have an eye for design, beautiful things, balance, and harmony.

Social Driving Force

People who have a strong social driving force have a genuine interest in others. They appreciate people and are often considered friendly, sympathetic, and unselfish. They can sometimes consider those with strong theoretical, practical–economic, and aesthetic driving forces cold and impersonal. People with a distinct social driving force are often self-sacrificing by nature.

Individualistic Driving Force

People motived by this driving force are concerned with power, whatever their field. Research has shown that leaders in most industries have a strong individualistic driving force. Many philosophers have argued that power is the most universal and most fundamental driving force, since competition and struggle are inevitable parts of life. In some people, this trait is especially dominant. These people often strive for personal power, influence, and success.

Traditional Driving Force

This driving force is focused on maintaining a strong sense of tradition and has a deep loyalty to the historic order of things. Individuals with a strong traditional driving force feel most comfortable in structured environments and often enjoy being part of organizations they believe in and that offer guidelines for how they should live their life. This isn't necessarily a religious faith. It could be any type of group or organization, such as a political party or something less structured—like the vegan community—as long as it provides clear rules and principles for how one ought to live.

You probably recognized yourself in some of the examples above, but not in all of them. Typically, a person has two driving forces that dominate their behavior, but there are many exceptions to that rule. The key takeaway is that there are only a handful of powerful driving forces that motivate people's behavior. Some psychologists maintain that there are only two major driving forces: power and sex. (Or, as somebody said: Everything is about sex—except sex. Because that is about power. Think about it!)

A Simple Example from Real Life

Regardless of what our driving force is, we will strive after whatever our driving force is in every aspect of our lives, and sometimes we're willing to cross a few lines to get it. You can use yourself as an example. The choices you make reflect who you are and what you value. If you're asked to choose between a free yearlong gym membership on the one hand, or a year's worth of free chocolate and sweets on the other, which would you choose? Pretend both are worth about a thousand dollars, so it isn't about money.

"The gym membership," you might say. Apart from that being a healthier answer, it would be reasonable to assume that you have chosen it because you like to stay in good shape and you think you'll live longer if you eat fewer sweets and exercise more. You'll definitely reduce the risk of developing health complications related to being overweight. But at the same time, we know that it isn't quite that simple. The receptors in the brain are often what govern simple decisions. How quickly will I get my reward? If I take the chocolate, I'll have it in one minute; with a gym membership, it might take six months before I see any real results. In this case, the driving forces are a combination of pleasure and character. Because we all know what the "smart" decision is.

When It's Not that Simple

But what if you're thinking of getting a new job? Perhaps you've been offered your dream job, but the salary is just okay. At the same time, you have the chance of landing another job that seems perfectly okay and would mean a huge raise. Which would you choose? The dream job or the dream salary? It's easy in theory: the dream job. But we both know that real life doesn't work like that. Not everyone is driven by money, but many people are. It isn't a question of right or wrong; it just comes down to the power of your driving force. What motivates my decision?

Our driving forces decide many of our choices in life. When our driving force is being fulfilled, we feel content. Our driving forces are also critical when it comes to manipulation. Anyone who understands what motivates us is able to use this knowledge to further their own agendas.

People who manipulate others often do so for one of two reasons: to earn money or to acquire power. It's as simple as that. If you and I are driven by different things than money or power—for example, by wanting to help others or to create a better world—then we will be the ones who are exploited.

6

What Manipulation Looks Like

A man is never more truthful than when he acknowledges himself a liar.   —Mark Twain

As I have shown, influence does not always have to be negative. It's something we do all the time. Some people have described this as selling to each other: We sell each other thoughts, ideas, experiences, views, and opinions. This happens all the time in bars and pubs—so I am told. Women and men try to convince strangers they've just met that they're the perfect partner.

Below are examples of behaviors that can be used for good or for deceitful purposes, depending on the circumstances.

So how could a person of each color convince you to invest money, change your job, go on a trip with them that you have reservations about, or even just make dinner tonight even though it's not your turn? What behaviors are YOU especially sensitive to? Do you react favorably if somebody gets straight to the heart of the matter and simply says what they want? Or would you much rather be charmed and delighted? Do you prefer strong, silent types, people who don't talk about themselves but ask insightful questions about you? Perhaps you're the no-nonsense type who really appreciates competent people.

HIGH D/RED	HIGH I/YELLOW	HIGH S/GREEN	HIGH C/BLUE
Dominant	Inspiring	Stable	Analytical
Proactive	Extroverted	Patient	Investigative
Ambitious	Persuasive	Reliable	Cautious
Strong-willed	Verbal	Attentive	Systematic
Problem solver	Open	Restrained	Precise
Energetic	Positive	Lovable	Logical
Competitive	Empathetic	Persevering	Conventional
Forceful	Optimistic	Good listener	Distant
Inquisitive	Creative	Friendly	Objective
Direct	Spontaneous	Cautious	Perfectionist
	Sensitive	Supportive	

But regardless of what method is most effective, you need to know what your weakness is. You need to understand when other people are leading you to a choice you don't want to make. And you need to understand the method they will use to do it. Then you can choose whether to play along or not. It's important to ensure that whether you choose to play along or not, it is your choice and not the result of somebody leading you blindly. My thesis is simple: Nobody should be manipulated into doing something against their will. You need to be aware of what is happening around you.

Here are a few examples of tricks and methods that people of various colors can use to influence others. We'll go through the colors one by one, starting with Red behavior.

How a Red Will Influence You

You can't miss it. The Red simply tells it the way it is: Their idea is better than the one you just put forward. The advantages are obvious;

if you don't understand that, then you're just slow. Red behavior is simple and direct. Normally, they can't be bothered to make cunning plots or pull strings. Nor do they beat around the bush. They explain their idea and its benefits and expect you to say yes.

Of course, even Red people can sometimes act manipulatively, but for the most part they don't have time for that.

The Red Seller

An example: Robert is a sales rep for a pharmaceutical company. He visits a doctor who hasn't bought anything from his company before. Since Robert's employer, Big Pharma, Ltd., is threatening to replace Robert if sales figures don't improve, he decides to ignore all the selling models and lovely presentations. Instead, he is going to be outspoken and tell the doctor that he just needs to be logical and see the advantages of his product. Convinced that this meeting is going to go brilliantly, he steps into the doctor's office, explains the new super product, and finishes by saying that the doctor should start using it immediately. The patients will get better quicker, and everything will be fantastic! The clinical studies all show this, and if the doctor can't see that, then Robert will be happy to talk to someone higher up. Because obviously the doctor is going to think rationally when he makes his choice. He certainly isn't going to allow himself to be influenced by the fact that he has a good relationship with the sales rep from a competitor.

The doctor could very well buy from Robert because of this method. Robert, who is Red, has shown that he is bold: He has bypassed all the classic selling blurb, and it's likely that he will get through to the doctor. A lot of people like sellers who are prepared to challenge their customers.

I belong to that category of buyers. I like it when people stand up for themselves and state things plainly. It shows that they respect me and are there to do business. Because I am, too.

Dealing with a Red Person Who Tries to Sell to You

If you are a customer standing in front of an intense Red seller who has not convinced you in the slightest, then just say no, maybe raising your voice slightly. You might have to say no loud and clear, but nobody can actually force you to buy something you don't want. If the Red seller is decently intelligent, they'll get the message. If they're at the end of their sales cycle and need to clock up a few extra deals before the end of the month, then they'll try again. And again. To be honest, they will push you fairly hard to try to get you to say yes.

Stand firm. If you don't want what they are selling, say "No thank you." Then leave. That's right. You leave the premises, the meeting room, or whatever. You don't have to sit there and play along and be polite when you're dealing with a Red seller. You do, however, have to indicate that the exchange is over. The Red seller will let go of you and your bad judgment and move on to the next customer. I'm not saying that you should be an insensitive jerk, but I think you understand what I mean. Just leave.

But what about at home?

In the context of a personal or private relationship, it's harder to get off the hook. If your Red wife looks you right in the eye and says "we're going to the Caribbean this Fall," then you have a much bigger problem. Sometimes you simply have to surrender and go on the trip. Or visit your mother-in-law. Or go to another brewery. Or sit through the symphony again. Small compromises in a marriage are normal and healthy. It's a way to adjust, and we all have a responsibility to be generous to one another. In the best-case scenario, you're living with someone with whom you share interests. But if you're faced with a situation that you really can't tolerate, then you need to do something.

It might be that your wife wants to go snorkeling in the Caribbean, but you have two serious objections. One is that you don't actually like snorkeling at all. You're all for a vacation with sun and sand, but snorkeling is a bit frightening because you tried before and it didn't go very well. You got a skin rash, you were attacked by something with scales, and it is not an experience you want to repeat. The other reason could be that you think it's too expensive. A holiday in the Caribbean for the whole family will eat up too much of your savings. Your Red wife can be a bit shortsighted and wants to use every single cent in the budget. It's just money, after all; you can always get more. But you know that your car is on its last legs, and the fridge is making ominous noises, too.

A vacation—or an expensive dinner out or front-row tickets to the game, whatever it may be—is a tricky situation, since nobody wants to be called a bore or a stick-in-the-mud or whatever else a Red person can think up in the heat of the battle. But remember that Red people are often in the habit of kicking up a bit of a fuss to get what they want. They're not afraid of conflict, and you shouldn't be either. If you think that you have good, concrete reasons why you shouldn't take a trip to the Caribbean, then try the following:

1. Write down all the facts: the logistics, the cost—everything that is affected by the decision. Compare the cost and value of this trip with choices you two have made previously (say, the cost of getting something repaired at home or for childcare). This will slow down the Red, who might get angry about your frustrating focus on details. When a Red wants something, a Red wants it deeply and knows exactly what you're trying to do.

2. Demand to be shown the details; this is what Reds fear the most. Weigh all the pros and cons. Your spouse will list all the pros they can think of; you'll have to supply the disadvantages. Sometimes you'll discover that your spouse is right, that the advantages do outweigh the disadvantages, and that's great, because then you do

get to go to the Caribbean. But sometimes the reverse will be true. If you can put up with your spouse's bad mood and impolite way of talking to you, you can get them to digest the facts.

3. Refuse to listen to angry outbursts. Point to the facts time after time. Be consistent. Keep repeating yourself until your spouse understands that you're not going to give in.

4. Red people hate to lose, so offer a compromise. Grant a concession so that the Red can still feel they have won. Perhaps a long weekend at Myrtle Beach? The household budget can cope with that, and there's a beach in South Carolina, too.

5. Buy flowers.

The Yellow's Method to Make You Buy Shit You Really Don't Need

I'll save you time and remind you that Yellow behavior is often the most manipulative. Why is that? Yellows have the gift of the gab. Everything they say sounds good. They're skilled at communicating and clever at making people like them. And why not? The Yellow person is happy, laughs a lot, and likes to joke and fool around. They create a lovely mood wherever they go. What is there to dislike?

If a Yellow wants you to go along with something you're not keen on, they'll do several things. To start with, they'll flatter you. Yellow people like to give out compliments. And they might be absolutely honest compliments. They might really like your new jacket or think you are good at talking to a group. But they also know the value of praising people, even when it's obvious that they want something.

The Yellow Persuader

Lisette is a real estate agent. She's amazingly successful in her field. When she wants to sell you a far too expensive apartment, she'll manage it by making use of the so-called similarity effect. If she sees that your handbag is Louis Vuitton, she'll say that she's thinking of buying a similar handbag. If she finds out that you have a cat, she will absolutely ADORE cats (or switch cats for dogs, guinea pigs, geckos, or any pet you can name). And she will smile nonstop.

Once you find yourself really liking Lisette, she'll describe the view from the apartment. What it looks like outside, how it sounds—she'll even ask you who you want to invite to your housewarming party. Can you imagine standing on the balcony and watching the sun set across the city with a glass of champagne in your hand as your friends congratulate you on having bought this fantastic apartment?

And, in fact, you can. It sounds absolutely wonderful. Soon you'll know exactly what you're going to wear to the party. You can see the apartment full of your relatives, and wouldn't it be fun to see the look on your father-in-law's face when he sees this place? Lisette is good at creating images inside your head. She speaks metaphorically and looks so enthusiastic you'll start wondering why she hasn't put in an offer on the apartment herself.

Is this manipulation or just ordinary sales talk? If you're being attentive, you'll be able to see the difference. This is what the real estate agent makes her living doing. You could say it's part of the social contract between you and her. Both of you know what's happening: You know that she is going to do everything she can to get your signature on a piece of paper. And she knows that you don't expect anything less. We know that she's just doing her job.

This is just how a Yellow person is going to sell to you. If it feels good—buy! If you feel that something isn't quite right—don't buy. Simple, right?

How to Keep a Yellow Seller at Bay

As you will have realized, there is a reason why lots of Yellow people work in some kind of sales job. They are gifted speakers, and they are good at opening doors. They'll talk with anybody. They have a charisma that doesn't seem forced and that leaves you feeling great. So how do you defend yourself?

Just like with the Red seller, you can very simply say you aren't interested. But since you've read this far, I'm guessing that you think really pushy sellers are a bit of a pain. And you don't want to create a tense situation.

Yellow sellers are less inclined to stick to details and facts than the other colors. That sort of thing bores them, and it's normally fairly easy to catch a Yellow seller getting something wrong. An easy way to do this is to just ask for some good, hard facts. With a real estate agent, there are lots of ways to make them show their hand.

Let's say that you don't want to have this apartment pushed on you or that you simply want to look around in peace and quiet. Try to ignore the emotional attraction of the elegant apartment. Instead, ask some detailed questions. What is the total square footage, and where is the floor plan? How much was the apartment sold for the last time it changed owners? Has the housing association created a fund for repairs, and how much money is in it? Can you arrange a private viewing at ten o'clock in the evening when your uncle comes to town?

You get the idea. You can carry on like that until the real estate agent decides to hand you an information sheet or just gives up. Maybe she'll move on to the next prospective buyer who seems less critical. She sees all of your impertinent questions as criticism of the apartment, the housing association, the whole area, and who knows—maybe the real estate agent herself? Now you can think in peace and quiet without having her hanging over your shoulder and whispering fairy tales into your head with all her talking.

But What if I Live with a Super Talker?

When it comes to relationships, things are a lot more difficult. If you have a Red partner, you can disagree, loudly, and if you can handle being in the center of the storm for a while, then the problem is usually solved. But with Yellows . . . all that persuasive ability and energy, combined with an extravagant emotional life . . .

Your Yellow husband wants to start a new project: Build a garage! You put your hand on your forehead and look out the window, where your eyes fall on a number of other projects he has undertaken: an apple tree that has partly been dug up, a half-painted fence, a deck with half the planks missing and no railings, an unmowed lawn that has a gigantic hole in the middle of it—and you can't even remember what that hole was supposed to be.

The easiest thing would be to say, "Sure, go ahead and build it." But you know that your husband, a happy, positive, and very sympathetic guy, never actually finishes anything—ever (see Yellow behavior—weaknesses). So you can't just say "go ahead." The thought of yet another unfinished project gives you a headache, and he hasn't even started yet. You know that building a garage is going to be far too expensive, that it won't ever be finished, that it's almost winter, that you never even wanted a garage, much less needed one. This is not a debate on the usefulness of a garage but a situation where you do not want to be persuaded to go along with something against your wishes.

I recommend that you take a risk. Sit down, breathe calmly, and act enthusiastic. It would be great to have a garage! How lovely to have the car in there in the winter so you won't have to scrape ice off the windshield! (Although you already know that the garage isn't for the car, but for some other not-yet-started project.) It's important that you display enthusiasm for the idea; otherwise, he won't listen to you. If you start off by saying, "But really James, another project?" he'll only get stubborn. Instead, ask him to tell you how he envisions the new garage. Show that you're interested in what it's going to look like. Where he's going to build it. What color it's going to be. He'll give you lots of details, and his imagination will run wild.

And what do you do? You smile and nod.

Then you take your hubby on a tour of the yard and the garden. You tell him that a garage would be amazing because it would help to keep things neat and organized. He is going to nod, still just as enthusiastic. Now you're standing on the site of the future garage. He shows you where it will stand and describes it. You might even give each other a celebratory hug, since you're both so excited for the project.

Now you take him to the unfinished deck on the other side of the house and let him have a look at its sorry state. The railings, too. Then you walk across to the hole with the forgotten purpose in the middle of the lawn, the hole that three-year-old Philip fell into last spring and hurt himself. Now you tell James that you absolutely love the idea of a garage and that once the railings, and the decking, and the abyss in the lawn, and all the rest of the half-finished projects are completed, you'll happily help him build a garage. In fact, you promise to drive every single screw by yourself.

You probably understand the psychology here, but to make it clear: You never say *no* to a garage. He hasn't agreed not to build one, and you haven't suggested at any point that you don't like the idea of one. You've actually delivered a resounding *yes* to the idea of a new garage. You just want him to finish the other projects first. But both of us know that this isn't going to happen anytime soon.

Who knows? If he does manage to sort out all the other things, you might decide you actually *want* a garage.

The challenge with Yellow partners is that they are easily offended. It's always risky to criticize their ideas. They will see you as negative and limiting. So you should smile throughout the entire conversation. Smile and nod, but make your point of view known.

It's more about how you present something than what you actually say.

How Greens Will Appeal to Your Soft Heart

Sometimes I feel a bit sorry for really Green people. They're so careful and so considerate that it's hard to believe that any of them would ever force an opinion or anything else on someone who doesn't want it. Being the good team players that they are, the team will always take precedence over the individual. At least most of the time.

Even a Green person has methods to get you where they want you. But their methods look extremely different. The Green approach is to never say straight out what it is they want. Instead, they hint at things; plant a tiny, tiny seed of an idea; and hope you will guess what it is. Since Green people are the opposite of confrontational, they make use of a technique that appeals to your emotions.

Imagine a ten-year-old child who has everything he needs. Nice clean clothes, food on the table, his favorite dessert whenever he asks for it. He prefers to be inside and amuse himself playing some type of computer game, watching TV, or reading a book. Every time his parents tire of this—usually during the summer—and want to restrict his computer gaming or TV watching, they demand that he goes outside for a while. The reaction? Objections and a doomsday look on his face. The child doesn't confront his parents directly. He is perfectly aware of the fact that he hasn't seen daylight for a week, but he has such a miserable look that you would think he's been gravely mistreated. Nothing is fun anymore. His head droops and he hardly answers you. He has difficulty getting his food down. The apocalypse is just around the corner. He does this to make you feel guilty for your horrible cruelty. This is what psychologists call passive-aggressive behavior. And somehow he manages to persuade his parents to buy even more computer games—all by making himself look like a victim.

A victim of *what*, you might be wondering? A victim of the terrible circumstance of not having that game he has wanted for so long. The one everyone else already has. If you're a parent, you'll recognize the situation. Sometimes you give in because you feel guilty. You don't want to see your kid suffer.

Now translate this to an adult. If the method that gets the ten-year-old what he wants actually works, why change that method as an adult? The Green seller always looks as if they have had a bit of a rough time compared with the charismatic Yellow, with their broad smile, or the forceful Red, with their firm handshake. The Green doesn't have the drive or the energy that comes naturally to the other two. So, instead, the Green appeals to your emotions.

The Green Car Salesman

Green car salesman Greg wanted me to buy a new station wagon. It was fairly expensive, with a lot of extras. I didn't want a station wagon. I wanted a sedan. Greg's first move was to shake his head to indicate how wrong I was. What about all the family holidays? Didn't I realize that everybody needed to have plenty of room for their stuff? The children's bicycles (children, always the children; if you want to guilt someone into something, use the children as leverage), your wife's extra suitcase, just in case she needs to have a fancy outfit. And didn't we have a dog? If not, I should get a dog. Kids love dogs.

I know why none of this worked on me, and I'll come to that. But then he started on my interests. Did I play golf? Go windsurfing? Cycling? The answers were all no, so what on earth did I do in my free time? I write, I answered, and my computer case hardly takes any room at all.

Greg hinted that I was a first-class narcissist. It was clear that I was only thinking of myself. I explained that I had recently got divorced and that my children were more or less grown up. For a while he tried to use what he considered a logical argument, but one I found rather childish: *Everybody else buys the station wagon.*

That argument was totally wasted on me, because it would never occur to me to buy something just because everybody else does. To the extent that it's possible to be unique in this society, I'd like to try. I explained this to him, probably sounding slightly irritated because I thought that he hadn't paid any attention to what I needed in a car.

Then he just sort of physically deflated and mumbled an apology. How could he have been so stupid? No wonder things weren't going well for him, I heard him say. I can only assume that this was also a selling tactic, but it didn't work well on me. He ought to have inflated my ego and explained that I would look much better in the sleeker station wagon than in the sedan version of the same model.

How to Avoid Feeling Sorry for this Guy

How much do you care about the Green person's feelings? If you can answer that question, then you already know the solution to the problem. Just like with the Red and the Yellow sellers, it's extremely simple to just say "no thank you, I am not interested."

The Green person doesn't use the same pressure tactics as the Reds or Yellows and doesn't push the deal along like those colors do; instead, they behave much more passively. They hope you will buy the car without their needing to argue the case. (I once met a Green seller who claimed that he never asked the customer to seal the deal. I asked him why. He answered that it was just too unpleasant to be told "no.") You can simply ask for time to think about it and just walk away. They aren't going to chase you through the showroom waving their order book.

So, how much do you care about the Green person's feelings? Buying from somebody just because you feel sorry for that person has never seemed to me to be a sustainable system, but we're all different. When it comes to an actual salesperson, it's very simple to say no and walk away from that person's disappointment.

But let's say that the Green individual is your partner. Your husband or wife. It's similar to the garage-building Yellow husband with the delicate feelings, but much worse. But we don't want to create conflict, just ensure (in a friendly, firm way) that we are not backed into a corner we don't want to be in. And to show that we're not fooled by the methods some people resort to.

It's typical for Green people to try to manipulate or influence the rest of us by doing absolutely nothing. If you think about it, it's possible to prevent almost anything by simply digging in and just refusing to play along. Imagine a motorway where the speed limit is sixty-five miles an hour. Two lanes, but nothing is moving. For mile after mile. A single car that has broken down can cause total chaos.

Your Stubborn Hubby at Home

It works just the same way with Green partners. The man who didn't want to go with you to the family reunion dinner has his own method of getting you to cancel (and that's what it's usually about—something the Green does NOT want).

He won't tell you that he doesn't want to go. He won't say that he'd rather stay at home and watch football (just like the last 333 Saturdays). Instead, he'll say that he doesn't feel so well. When you ask him what the trouble is, the answer will be rather vague. Stomach pains, headache, or he'll just be feeling—err—a bit off.

The fact is that you—if you haven't anticipated this—now have a problem because your husband has decided to be obstructive and not play along. He wants to hear you voluntarily say that you can both stay at home. But tonight you would really like to join the family for dinner. Some cousins are coming and it's been ten years since you last saw them. This is important to you. And you want your husband to go with you.

It seems you have three options:

1. Do what he wants and stay at home. Achieve a temporary calm but regret it for months.
2. Go to the family reunion dinner on your own, since your

husband is going to huff and puff and act as if life is miserable. And he'll want to go home early anyway.

3. Or you can take him with you and simply not care what he thinks. You can always argue until he gives in, and I'm guessing you already know how to do that.

Forget all the above. The solution is something entirely different. If you know your husband and can see the pattern of how he manipulates you to get his own way, then when you first tell him about the reunion, you'll already know what will happen in six weeks. You can prepare yourself for his opposition by planning in advance. Because even if he says yes to the dinner when you mention it the first time, you know there are still risks. He *always* says yes at first. (Although "yes" sounds more like "that shouldn't be a problem," or "that's worth thinking about," or you might just get an "ummm" in answer.)

Step by step over the next six weeks leading up to the reunion dinner, you can build up your husband's desire to come along. You bring up everything that is positive: Your brother is going to be there and he and your husband have always gotten along well, the food will be amazing—it's his favorite restaurant—and you can always record the football game. With a bit of effort, he'll have a positive attitude and put on his best shirt without the slightest grumble.

But it would be better still if you confront him about his reluctance to leave the house. Remind him how important this reunion is for you. Force him to agree to the fact that you must attend the reunion and that you want him to be with you. Remind him of similar situations where he refused point-blank. Discuss calmly and methodically what happened: how he felt when he first said yes, and why he had probably meant no the entire time. Ask him if that stomachache was just pretense or if it was nerves. That would be perfectly reasonable; we've all felt nervous facing our spouse's family.

But talk about the actual problem!

Explain that you see through his stubbornness and that even though you love him, you don't want to be manipulated. Get him to promise that he won't try any tricks on the day of the family reunion. And remind him about that several times, until Saturday comes along.

I can almost hear what you are thinking now: *Why should I have to treat a grown-up man like he's a child?!?*

Just like the ten-year-old with the computer games and TV watching, your Green husband will use the methods he knows work. This is still passive-aggressive, although it's the adult variety. He won't change his attitude until you actively show that you're immune to it. You need to get him to communicate about the issue rather than allowing him to stubbornly stay sitting on the sofa drinking beer, watching football, and grumbling about a bad call.

It's entirely up to you.

How Blues Will Convince You with Just the Facts

How to Be Convincing with Factual Arguments

In recent years I have met sellers in every field you can imagine. I've met them through various development programs, and I dare say that there is no type that I haven't come across. The (statistically) most common color in a sales team is Yellow, and many of them are sharp sellers. But some of the real stars that I've met, those notorious overachievers who exceed their budget targets year after year, almost always have a fair dose of Blue in them, too. I'd say there are two reasons for this. First, they're extremely structured in their way of working. And, second, they stick to facts.

You probably won't be impressed by the Blue seller's charisma and enthusiasm. (As usual, there are exceptions.) But you will be impressed by how they work.

The Blue Businesswoman

Sara has sold kitchens for many years. She is known for her attention to detail and her calmness. When you and your husband visit the showroom, she'll notice all the details about you: how you're dressed, what your wedding ring most likely cost—everything. Unlike the Yellow seller, Sara isn't going to chatter on and on, and she won't say that she loves Chanel. But she will recognize Chanel when she sees it. And she'll register it in her encyclopedic brain.

You sit down, and Sara will start asking questions. She'll address herself to both of you equally. Are you here to order a kitchen *today*? What type of kitchen? Any favorite materials? Are there any basic requirements or absolute no-no's? What works well in the kitchen you have now? What's missing? The list is going to be long, and you might find Sara a little exhausting. You'll want to feel the countertops, choose the cupboard doors, and all those fun things. But this is Sara's analysis of your needs. She always works like this, and her BMW outside the showroom (which she didn't need to borrow money to buy) is proof that she knows what she is doing.

Not until she thinks she knows who you are, what your budget is, and how urgent things are will she take you to the display units to choose materials and finishes and all the rest. You might not be inspired by her matter-of-fact calmness, but you will receive answers to all your questions. Because Sara knows her stuff. There isn't much she has to look up. She can rattle off the technical details of every stovetop in the showroom.

You won't order your new kitchen on this first visit. A completely new kitchen in an average-sized house or apartment is a major expense. We're talking lots of money. You'll want to take the plans home with you so you can discuss them. Sara knows that. So she won't try to clinch the deal straightaway; rather, she will send you home with lots of pamphlets about the design package she's put together for you. But you can be sure she will have noted down your cell phone numbers and your email addresses.

Because Sara is going to call you the next day and ask how you feel about the kitchen designs. She'll ask if you were satisfied with the package or if there's anything you'd like to change. And if you say you want to think about it a bit more, she will phone you the following day. And the day after that. In fact, she will follow up until you finally say yes to the package, or no thank you. That is the Blue seller's foremost strength—they don't let go.

Of course, this isn't a form of manipulation; it's just an extremely effective way of doing business. But you should know that it's a bit like dealing with a badger. It will bite hard. It won't let go. And it won't be easy to shake off.

How to Survive the Structure Queen

This isn't anything you need to make a fuss about. The Blue seller doesn't have the challenging manner of the Red, they don't fire off a barrage of words like the Yellow, and they won't appeal to your conscience like the Green. Blue people try to be extremely rational. They look at the sale as a challenging problem and try to solve it logically—the same way Sara sells kitchens. How do you avoid ordering your new kitchen from her in particular? If it's because you don't like Sara, or that the kitchen plan she put together turned out far too expensive, or that you simply weren't in love with the design, or you have a better deal from another supplier, then just say so.

Say: "I don't want this kitchen. Thanks for your time; I'll get back to you if I change my mind."

Simple, right? The Blue seller, like the Red one, will be disappointed at having lost a deal, but she won't be hurt or offended. She knows that this is part of the business. Most proposals result in a no. (In fact, in all selling activities, you hear a lot more no than yes.)

Blue sellers generally follow the rule book. If you say that you don't want to be contacted again, you probably won't be. But if the seller says that they'll phone you next week and you say sure, then you'll be hearing from them next week. That's how they function. If you find it hard to say no but want to say no, do it as soon as possible. It saves everybody's time.

So What Does Life Look Like with a Blue Partner?

Let's go back to personal relationships. Say that your partner is bright Blue and comes up with an idea you don't like at all. They want to quit their job and go back to school again. (Blue people are quite often dedicated readers and like to absorb lots of facts.) Your partner comes to you with a plan—naturally—and has worked out just exactly how many course credits are needed and how long it will take to get them. They already know exactly which job they could realistically expect to land after getting these new qualifications. Perhaps they've even worked out a financial plan, since your joint income is going to decrease dramatically during the next two years.

This is a tricky situation that can lead to a very tense discussion. On a purely intellectual level, you understand that your partner is right: If they get a new degree, then they can get a job that would be more satisfying than the job they have now. Their salary would also be 25 percent higher—after two years, and assuming they get a new job. But it also means you would be pretty hard up until then. You are very worried about your finances already, and the thought of only having one income makes you panic. You might have to borrow money. It just seems impossible.

Sure, there can be other, more selfish reasons for you not to want to support your partner's plan. Perhaps you feel insecure about them eventually making more than you. Perhaps you don't want to have more household duties. You might even mention that the kids will miss having both parents at home on class nights. God forbid, these evening classes might even restrict your ability to pop down to the sports bar to watch the game. So maybe you're just an ass. None of those motives are especially noble, but let's say that you think you have a good reason to object to the idea.

Your partner is acting rationally and logically. They're not trying to manipulate you at all—that's not typical Blue behavior—but they quite clearly want to influence you. The logic and calculations will be unassailable.

The counterweapon is strong emotions. An outbreak of anger. Tears. Behave as irrationally as possible. This might very well put your partner off-balance. Blue people think more than most people. They will analyze you and decide if you're just acting or whether your concern is genuine—if they think it is, then they'll listen and put forward solutions.

A better method, however, is to negotiate. If you go along with their plan, what can they do in return? If they are going to be off at classes so and so many hours a week while you run the household, what will you get in return? This is most definitely playing dirty, but if you don't want to go along with the whole thing, you don't need to do anything. And what would your new higher joint income be used for, once it comes? You've always wanted to travel to the Bahamas: Would your partner entertain the idea of celebrating their new job with a fancy trip for the whole family? Or can you save the money for the children's education?

The advantage to Blue behavior is that these people often remember what you have agreed to before. Their brains are extremely well organized, and they will know what's going on. Blue people can, of course, be emotional about this or that, but they are fairly rational.

But that also means that if you succeed in your negotiation and get your partner to delay going to school for a year, in exactly one year they'll be planning to go. And then you had better have new, really good arguments, or—hopefully—have changed your mind.

7

The Dominant Red Psychopath

Psychopaths act out their lunatic thoughts while the
rest of us just think them. —Marty Rubin

Okay, now we've looked at how influence or manipulation or even
ordinary everyday salesmanship can affect our decisions. But so far
I've mainly dealt with examples of influence where there isn't a hidden agenda, where there are no malevolent ulterior motives. Speaking
of agendas . . . there are a number of different types of agendas. We
shall take a closer look at them.

1. OPEN AGENDA THAT WE HAVE BOTH AGREED ON

Before you exclaim, "That car salesman certainly had an agenda
of his own—he bloody well wanted to sell me a car!" I'd remind you
that we already *know* that a seller or a real estate agent is there to sell
or to negotiate a sale. Like I said before: Their motives are completely
open; nothing about their roles is hidden from anybody. If the real
estate agent had claimed that she only wanted to find the very best
apartment for your family and had nothing to gain from the sale,
then that would be a different situation. If she had immediately suggested an apartment she had just been commissioned to sell—or her
own apartment—then we could question how neutral she really is.
With the housing market the way it is in major cities, you can indeed

start wondering who the real estate agent is working for: the buyer or the seller. But we all understand her role is to make sure that houses and apartments change hands.

2. HIDDEN AGENDA THAT WE'VE BOTH AGREED ON

The way banks function is worse. They're not as honest about what they do. Since my résumé includes fourteen years of working in banks, I am taking the liberty of being honest on this point. Bank salespersons have never actually been called salespersons. They're called financial advisor or personal investment strategist or agent or whatever, but never salesperson. But in principle that's what they actually do: They sell. And we fall into the trap every time, because they only suggest their own products. This system has been criticized for years, with good reason, but nothing has been done to alter it. The bank managers themselves have essentially no say in how things are run, so there's no point going to your local bank and raising a fuss. But keep in mind that they are all salespersons, not advisors. This is an example of a hidden agenda that is mutually agreed on. There is a hidden agenda—the bank's desire to sell their financial products to you—that we all know about and have allowed to exist.

3. HIDDEN AGENDA THAT IS ACTUALLY HIDDEN

When we talk about people who have a hidden agenda, a completely different purpose than the one they say they have, we're talking about psychological manipulation with malevolent intentions. Normal people, you and me and most of the people we are ever going to meet, find it hard to imagine that someone out there would do the things we ourselves are not capable of. Sure, we're not naïve. We know all about psychopathic dictators. We know about vicious serial killers. We've read about them. But we often imagine them to be just as monstrous in their everyday behavior as they are when they are

committing gross atrocities. We think that people who commit geno-
cide can't also take their car to the car wash and pick up some milk on
the way home. And that is a mistake that is dangerously far from the
truth. The worst monsters have learned to behave just as normally as
you and me. Some of them can even seem so normal that it makes us
look like the deviant ones. And that's where the challenge lies.

The people we will now look at are the ones who can't be categorized in the DISC system. They are the people without a color, the
ones with every color, the fifth color. The evil distortion of you and
me. The psychopaths.

It's the Red Who's the Psychopath!

To be honest, the head above is a fairly common remark I hear when
I am lecturing at different organizations. Since strictly Red behavior
is so rare (0.5 percent of the population have *only* Red in their profile),
there are a lot of people who don't understand them. To be arguing
one second, then to invite you to lunch the next second—that seems
totally weird, doesn't it?

If I was given a dollar every time a person came up to me and,
after discreetly looking to their right and left, explained that they seriously suspected that their boss could be a psychopath, well then I'd
be writing this book on a private island. After they've shared their
suspicion, I ask a few questions and the person describes their boss.
Angry, aggressive, just runs over everyone, doesn't listen, makes
unreasonable demands, requires total devotion to work, and never
hands out praise.

Sure, some reliable studies do indicate that the higher up you go in
an organization, the more psychopaths you're likely to come across.
But the same also applies to Red behavior.

Think about it. The higher you climb, the more the wind will blow. Everything is harder at the top. More competition, more responsibility, and higher stakes. Since Reds can deal with a slap in the face better than the other colors, they often end up in senior positions, thanks to their sharp elbows. It's lonely at the top, as the old saying goes.

Sure, but that doesn't mean they're not psychopaths.

What psychopaths have in common with Red people is that they can put up with those types of tough conditions. The psychopaths can endure because they don't care about others, and the Red people can persist because they are task- and issue-oriented and aren't particularly bothered by conflict. They're pragmatic and understand that not everyone will appreciate them. Of course, they'd prefer to be liked, just like everybody else, but they understand that's a fairy tale. So they steam ahead.

How Do I Distinguish a Psychopath from a Red Boss?

Interesting question. The Red boss can plow along like a steamroller, no doubt about that. The Red boss is going to tread on the toes of an awful lot of people and make some especially unpopular decisions for the purpose of achieving whatever their goal may be.

But they will be consistent. They will always be a bit tougher than average. They will also personally work very hard, which is an important clue. They'll often come first to work and be the last to leave. Which isn't at all what a psychopath would do. The psychopath's work ethic is totally different. They're only too happy to sneak away from anything that even looks like work.

Red bosses will not waste any time trying to charm their staff. This is a very important clue. Red people aren't typically relationship-oriented, and they can put up with the fact that others think all their unreasonable demands are a pain. This doesn't mean that they don't care about other people, but it definitely means that the job and the task take priority. First, work really, really hard; then celebrate with a dinner. Let's make sure that the finish line is in sight before we go off for long lunches and have a good time. They rarely take breaks—you won't find them sitting with a cup of coffee and chatting. They know that other people appreciate those coffee breaks, but since the chitchat isn't of any use to them, they simply skip it. So you'll rarely see them near the coffee machine.

In comparison, the psychopath takes part in social activities because they provide an opportunity to learn about the weaknesses of others—things that can be used against people whenever the psychopath gets the chance. And they will charm everyone they meet, at least at the beginning. You can say a lot about Red behavior, but you can't accuse them of ever trying to charm anyone.

So there is no overlap, right?

Stop there! There are definitely similarities between Red behavior and psychopathy. They both seem particularly insensitive, since they won't think twice about yelling at you for some silly trifle. Both Red bosses and psychopaths tend to criticize their staff in public.

With the Red, the victim may very well have deserved the criticism, and the boss is simply telling it how it is. This character trait is extremely unpleasant, but there's an essential difference between it and the conduct of a psychopath. The Red is aware of the fact that they sometimes annoy people with their dominant behavior, and even though that isn't their intention, they accept this consequence because they want to move forward. They often don't realize until afterward that somebody took a situation badly. But they'll just shrug their shoulders, because they hadn't intended to offend anybody. If people are going to be sensitive, then that's their problem!

When the psychopath tells someone off, they often do it because they take pleasure in seeing someone else feel embarrassed or hurt. It gives them extra energy, and they can often laugh at the misfortunes of others. The psychopath can always concoct a reason to start yelling. It just depends on how they feel at the time.

The psychopath's intentions are to damage and destroy individuals who seem susceptible to such treatment. They like to watch how people slowly break down under pressure.

The Takeaway

Do you see the difference? What we need to do is read the purpose behind a particular action. If we understand the reasoning behind it, we might have more patience with boorish Red bosses, and may even venture to let them know that telling off one of their team members is not okay.

But we should be extremely vigilant in watching for people who have psychopathic traits. They're not going to change their behavior, regardless of what you say. On the contrary, a psychopathic boss will deliberately continue their bad behavior if they know that you're offended by it. If you think you have a Red boss who might be open to straight talk and some firm feedback, there could be a problem if you tell them how their behavior has hurt you. If your boss is a psychopath and not a Red person, then you've just given them an effective weapon to use against you.

A Final Clue

Earlier, I mentioned work ethic. Red people, be they bosses or ordinary employees, work hard. Unless they have totally lost faith in the company or organization or would rather devote themselves to things they find more rewarding, they will put in the hours. Reds also tend to do most things themselves because they think they can do them better than anyone else. Many of them are utterly hopeless when it comes to delegating, since they don't trust their colleagues. This results in long workdays.

The psychopath, on the other hand, has no intention at all of doing the job themselves. They prefer to sneak away, delegate everything to anyone they can, and complain loudly if things don't go their way. They take long lunches, arrive late to work and leave early, and, when they finally realize that the deadline is only two days away, suddenly dump piles of work on their staff. Because the psychopath's ability to understand consequences is very limited, they often wait until the last minute to get things done. Then they will demand that everybody work round the clock until the job is done. And when the project is presented, the psychopathic boss will take credit for absolutely everything. They won't think twice about saying that it was thanks to their work that everything turned out as well as it did. After the staff had dawdled away and accomplished nothing, the psychopath had to step in and save the day.

Good Advice for All the Alphas

If you're Red, whether or not you're a boss, be conscious of the fact that people will give you funny looks if you come on too strong. Remind yourself that most people don't really understand your way of thinking. It might be a good idea to describe your intentions clearly so that you can avoid being called a psychopath behind your back.

8

The Charming Yellow Psychopath

Accuse the other side of that which you are guilty.

—Joseph Goebbels

At the risk of angering lots of Yellow people, I'll say it straight out: There are obvious similarities between Yellow behavior and psychopathic traits. According to Robert Hare's checklist, "glib and superficial charm" and "eloquence" are typical psychopathic traits. These traits describe too many Yellow people for us to ignore the similarity. Besides, Yellows are often seen as manipulative. They tend to make a show of their own importance, which is exactly what a true psychopath enjoys doing. In addition, Yellow people tend to blame others when everything starts to go wrong. Which is exactly what a psychopath does. This isn't a particularly flattering description of a person; I realize that. But why not call a spade a spade? Of course, Yellows also have a negative side. And in certain circumstances, the people around them will react strongly to their negative traits. Yellow people often don't notice this negative reaction because they don't pay attention to those around them. They talk on and use up all the oxygen in the room without realizing that other people just find it tiring.

Yellow people often tend to exaggerate their stories. In my previous book, *Surrounded by Idiots,* I told a story about an old mate,

Janne, who liked to embellish tales of his own experiences. He did so partly to make the stories more entertaining and partly to describe himself in more appealing terms. On one occasion, he told about a near-death experience when he and his wife had traveled by boat to a little island off the coast of Spain in the middle of a wild storm. His wife had already told me that they hadn't gone by boat at all but had flown, so I knew the story was made up. It was entertaining, no doubt about that, but it wasn't true. And when I confronted him with the facts, he got mad and clammed up completely.

Does this make Janne a psychopath? No, far from it. He simply likes to be entertaining, and in his enthusiasm to get people to laugh—or to be moved—he sometimes resorts to anecdotes that are not factual. Sure, he likes to be the center of attention. *All eyes on me* could be Janne's motto. And this irritates a lot of people, which is fair enough. But he is essentially harmless.

And—this is an important clue—he doesn't always lie. But when he's at a party, in fine form, hamming it up in front of a group of friends, then you absolutely need to take what he says with a grain of salt.

So How Do You Know if Someone is Telling a Story to Entertain or Is Lying Low to Be Deceitful?

Yellow behavior versus psychopathy. An interesting envisagement. There are two factors that can guide us: intention and frequency.

By "intention" I mean the purpose of a particular action. Why does Janne exaggerate his stories? What is the reason for this behavior? Does he want us to think he is bolder and more adventurous than he actually is so that we all stand in awe of him?

No. The main reason he resorts to this kind of lie is a lot simpler: He wants us to like him. And he wants to entertain us. Remember that Yellows view the people around them as their audience. The story with the boat that almost capsized far from land was fantastic. We laughed and came close to tears when he described the scene, so, yes, it was a good tale. Except for the annoying fact that it wasn't true.

Psychopaths have a different attitude toward lies. They lie because they like lying. They do it to test how far they can go. They find it amazing that other people actually believe them, and it amuses them to witness how gullible people can be. If I were to expose them and confront them with the lie, they would attack me straightaway. They'd point a finger and say that I'm the liar, that I'm the one who doesn't know what I'm talking about.

I have seen psychopaths look people in the eye and lie straight to their face without so much as blinking. Even when everybody, including the psychopath, knows that the lie has gone too far, the psychopath still doesn't stop. They won't admit anything. They keep going until they've confused everybody, and in the end nobody knows what to believe. It would be impressive if it weren't so vile.

But There Are Some Disturbing Similarities

The problem with psychopaths is that you can't tell when they're lying. A Yellow person becomes stressed and emotionally involved when they are exposed. They raise their voice and make even more of an effort, and their emotions become clearly visible. The Yellow person might stutter and get into a tangle, but the psychopath remains unmoved. The psychopath constructs increasingly elaborate lies until we are left totally confused, but the whole time the psychopath's pulse doesn't go up and they don't show any classic signs of lying, such as touching their face or neck. They just stand there and look as if they are the most credible person on the planet.

How can they be so unperturbed? Why don't they get nervous?

Because they don't feel anything. They feel no remorse for their lies, no empathy for those who are deceived—nothing.

The same applies to wanting to be the center of attention. Yellow people like being in the limelight, and it can be hard to get them to leave the stage. Psychopaths have a grandiose self-perception. They consider themselves more highly evolved than the rest of us, above the rest of us in an evolutionary sense. They put themselves in the center of things so that they can push aside everyone else and look like the most competent, intelligent person in a room.

I mentioned frequency as another important indicator. The Yellow is considered nice and charming when in their best mood. In more unfortunate moments, however, they can be extremely grumpy and irritated. When they are stressed, Yellow people can be hard to be around and are very far from charming. They become loudmouthed, complain incessantly, and blame everyone else without accepting responsibility.

How does the psychopath behave under stress? This is very interesting. Psychopaths don't seem to experience stress in the same way the rest of us do. The reason is that stress is typically connected with an emotion. For instance, it might be rooted in a fear of not succeeding, but psychopaths are incapable of feeling that fear. Stress is often the result of worrying too much about the opinions of others, but psychopaths do not care about others' opinions. They are confident from the beginning that they can handle anything, which means that they keep a cool head while normal people break down. On the battlefield, it's the psychopaths who take the greatest risks, because they enjoy the adrenaline kick they get from the danger.

Think about what usually makes you feel stressed. You work really hard all week and complete ninety-seven tasks of one hundred. It's finally Friday night, and you can go home. In the car or on the train, you think back about the last few days. What a week! Oh my God, such pressure! The stress you experience is not about the ninety-seven tasks you completed, but about the three you didn't have time to do. Normally, it isn't what *you have done* that causes stress, but what *you haven't done* that makes you worry.

A psychopath doesn't function like that. They don't care about what's on their to-do list. It doesn't bother them in the slightest, since they can always blame somebody else if a problem comes up.

The consequence is that the psychopath is always confident and appears in control. While the Yellow shows clear stress symptoms and can be short with others, since they can't keep up appearances, their psychopathic colleague is still positive. The psychopath is not affected by the circumstances, and they continue to charm their way through the office landscape while others are being smothered by the workload. This often means that psychopaths seem much more professional and competent to management. Despite the inhuman pressure, they are still on their feet. And smiling.

The bosses look at the psychopath and think: *What composure!* Maybe this guy is someone we should bring onto our management team!

But Nota Bene!

Frequency is a key factor here. The Yellows exaggerate (and perhaps lie) now and then. The psychopath lies *all the time*. About everything. Even when there's no reason to lie. They just do it.

The Yellow feels bad if they're confronted. They take criticism personally and will feel extremely uncomfortable for a time. The psychopath couldn't care less and just lies even more. If somebody approaches them with concrete facts—that everybody knows are correct—the psychopath has a plan for that, too. Regardless of the degree of criticism or confrontation, the psychopath just ignores it.

They might pretend to be offended and crushed by it, but only for show. It doesn't affect them in the slightest.

A Bit of Advice That Yellows Haven't Asked for, but Are Getting Anyway

There are important differences between Yellow traits and psychopathic ones. But if you are predominantly Yellow and are reading this: Know that you will sometimes be seen as exhausting and self-centered, even though that isn't your intention. You mean well, I know. The problem is that not everybody sees the difference. You need to realize that your exaggerations make other people distrust you. Your never-ending babbling gets on the nerves of most of the Reds and quite a lot of the Blues you meet. Other Yellows probably won't be provoked, since they themselves are too busy talking to hear what you're saying.

9

The Passive Green Psychopath

It isn't true that psychopaths never change. They change their mask and they change their target.

—Unknown

Umm, well, hang on a moment. What on earth could a Green do to be considered a psychopath? Has the author finally lost his marbles?

Let me explain.

Some time ago, I was invited to speak to a small group of managers who were interested in learning more effective communication tools.

When we come to the subject of weaknesses, I usually arrange an exercise where I ask people with the opposite qualities to describe each other's weak sides. This means that Reds get to describe the Greens and vice versa; the Yellows get to describe the Blues and vice versa. The fact that many (although not all) of the managers had Red traits in their personalities is not unusual, but it led to some unexpected effects.

When Green behavior was described, traits such as "unwillingness to change" and "stubbornness" came up. But even "afraid of conflict" and "dishonesty" turned up on the list. And this is interesting. We know that Greens don't like conflict, and even the Red person has noticed. Just looking a Green person in the eye is sometimes enough to land you in trouble with HR.

I talked with the group for a while about the reasons for this and the consequences. The Red perspective was that if you are really afraid of conflict, then you ought to do everything you can to avoid it. But the Green's way is to sweep the conflict under the rug, which simply ends up reinforcing the conflict. If it isn't dealt with, it gets bigger and finally threatens to explode in the Green's face.

I explained that Green persons tended to just push off unpleasant things, which is what they do to hide from conflict. But one man in the management group wouldn't give in: *They walk right into the conflict fully aware of what they're doing! They're psychopaths!*

Umm.

It's true that psychopaths often do things they know perfectly well don't work, but they always rely on their own ability to solve the problem whenever it arises. I simply have to confess: I hadn't thought about Green behavior in that way. When another man raised the question of dishonesty, the discussion got going.

My coworker was asked a simple question: Are you coming to the office party? He answered yes, even when I checked again with him to ensure that he really meant what he said. Yes every time. But it turned out that he had meant no the whole time.

Before I had time to respond, another Red manager exclaimed: *He lied to your face!*

So How Do We Know Which Is Which?

It shouldn't be that hard to tell a psychopath from a true Green because of the humble and friendly attitude that many Greens have, but for the sake of argument, let's look at the question. As I said earlier (and will say again): There are psychopaths, and there are people with psychopathic traits. One of these traits is, of course, manipulation.

While Yellow persons try to manipulate us fairly openly (*What a lovely sweater! Oh, by the way, could you help me with this report?*),

Green individuals have a completely different behavior. To the best of my knowledge, they are rarely called manipulative, but still Greens regularly manipulate quite a lot of people. The trick is that nobody—neither us nor them—realizes that's precisely what they're doing.

Imagine a situation where a group of old friends has planned a trip together. Perhaps it's friends from high school who reconnected at the reunion, and now they want to see each other more often. They are all enthusiastic and they've talked about the trip for several months. One of the people in the group has said the whole time that she will be going, but she hasn't taken an active part in the planning, she doesn't show any interest in the destination, and she hardly responds to emails. If directly asked about some detail, she always says yes. But that's all.

When the date for the trip creeps up, the group divides various logistical tasks among themselves, and the Green person is given the task of confirming the hotel reservation. They booked the rooms months ago, but it's important to double-check that all the rooms are grouped together.

The date of the trip arrives, and they all gather together at the airport, but they soon realize that somebody is missing. A certain person, who was quiet but promised that she would be coming, isn't there. The closer the plane gets to boarding, the more people in the group start worrying. Apart from the fact that it would be sad if she didn't come, she has booking confirmation from the hotel.

When someone finally manages to reach her by cell phone, she explains that she isn't feeling well and doesn't think she can come. When they ask about the hotel rooms, she responds vaguely that she never got a clear answer from the hotel staff.

Panic breaks out in the group. The whole vacation is at risk because they might not have anywhere to stay.

The inaction of the Green has had extreme consequences for a large number of people who trusted her from the very beginning. By simply delaying and not doing anything, she has put the group in a bad situation. They have been manipulated by their trust in a person who said one thing but meant another.

Maybe she did have malevolent intentions; perhaps she had a hidden agenda; perhaps she wanted to pay them back for some real or imagined injustice in the past; perhaps she had been bullied in school and now she has a bit of power; perhaps she simply didn't want to go on the trip. Or she was just a Green individual who was unwilling to act and, when confronted with responsibility, just pulled the covers over her head.

In this case, we're talking about a person who didn't actually want responsibility for anything. The problem was that she was so afraid of conflict that she never dared to just say "no thank you" to her enthusiastic former classmates. So she just sort of went along with it. But regardless of her intention by acting the way she did, she cheated the whole group out of their trip. Even though it looks different than other forms, this is a type of manipulation. Passive-aggressive behavior can have dramatic effects, even though you might not think about them that way.

So Do We Have a Real Psychopath Here?

This Green's behavior differs from that of the psychopath because she isn't entirely aware of what she is doing. *But hang on,* you might exclaim, *the Green person in the example knows exactly what she's doing. She was completely aware of the fact that her actions would cause trouble for a lot of people.* Yes, she probably was. But her defense mechanisms meant that she shut her eyes to the consequences of her choices. She was unable to contemplate the effects of her actions.

So What Have We Learned?

The psychopath is totally aware of what they're doing. If the Green considered the consequences of her inaction, it would be very cruel to let the whole group travel to Spain without having anywhere to stay. Wouldn't it?

The psychopath would probably be more active in tricking the group into trouble and would be aware they were doing so. The difference is that while the Green person will feel guilty about her behavior, the psychopath doesn't care that the vacation is ruined: It was the group's fault for being so stupid.

And that's how Green behavior works. They get others to do their job by always ducking. In the end, there is always somebody else who turns up and sorts out the things the Green didn't want to be bothered with.

A Piece of Advice for You Greens—and Listen Carefully Now, Because I Know You can

It probably hasn't occurred to you, but the fact is that you do actually manipulate others into various situations through your passive-aggressive behavior. To sneak away from responsibility is a psychopathic trait. And I know that you don't want to be thought of in that light. So think about how you can change your behavior in this respect.

Your group will come to appreciate you all the more if you are willing to be responsible.

To everybody else: Make sure that you keep track of who is tricking whom.

10

The Meticulous Blue Psychopath

I'm not a psychopath. I'm a high-functioning sociopath.
Do your research.   —Sherlock Holmes

In a word: No.

The Blue person is not easily perceived as a psychopath. I've never come across such a situation. A pedantic bureaucrat, sure. A slow person with a dreadfully boring obsession with detail, definitely. A perfectionist who sleeps with the rule book under their pillow and gripes about everyone else's low standards, yes, yes, of course.

But a psychopath? No, they're the last ones you would suspect.

Sure, we've all seen movies about the silent serial killer who never says a word. Who has everything at home in perfect order. Who sorts all those carved-out eyeballs in alphabetical order according to the victim's last name. But that's in the films, right? In real life, such behavior would be indicative of a severe personality disorder rather than Blue behavior.

There are, however, personality traits that can make it a challenge to distinguish Blue people from psychopaths. Imagine an extremely Blue person who doesn't have even a trace of Green or Yellow in their profile. They are not the slightest bit interested in relationships, and they think that people on the whole are rather a pain.

They prefer to spend all their time on their own and think that people talk too much.

How Does the Blue Behave?

In a very logical and clear-sighted manner. Uninterested in people and social dialogue, they answer in monosyllables. If you ask them for help, they'll say no, because you and your needs don't interest them. A lot of people perceive Blues as being unfeeling. They can look at you without moving a muscle in their face. They observe, judge, and analyze you without saying a word. And that's also what many psychopaths do. They stare at others like they are objects to be appraised. They often don't know when to look away or stop staring. Some researchers mention the "long" gaze that psychopaths have since they don't know when it is appropriate to look away. The staring is actually an indication of psychopathic behavior. Blue people can also get this wrong and stare at someone for an uncomfortable length of time.

Silence can also be difficult for people who are close to a Blue. Blue people don't feel the need to waste a single word unnecessarily. Even when they know the answer to a question, they may not share it because no one has asked them directly.

Psychopaths don't care about other people, and Blue people only care about a handful of their inner circle. If you are on the periphery of the Blue person's circle of acquaintances, they won't show much interest in you.

We Need an Example Here

I remember a story where a woman was being interviewed for a job she really wanted to get. The managing director was Yellow, smiled a lot, and was generally positive. The head of the finance department, who was also at the interview, hardly said anything, and his eyes barely moved. The woman began to feel a bit uncomfortable. After the interview, she had no idea how it had gone.

I've met all three people and it's always interesting to include this silent guy in a group. If you ask a question, he can look at you for a whole minute without saying a word. Then he'll give a slight nod. Well, okay then. This can definitely be off-putting to relationship-oriented people. Is it rude? Maybe not. But it is often perceived that way.

We often say it's the silent ones you need to keep an eye on. It's the distant, brooding figures who give no hint as to what is going on in their heads that we find most unnerving.

How Do I Know if I'm Dealing with a Psychopath or a Pedant?

A psychopath lies all the time without any clear motivation. Blues don't like to tell lies at all and prefer to answer truthfully when asked questions—however unpleasant the truth may be. Since they are rarely interested in your reaction to the unpleasant truth, they are willing to state the facts.

A psychopath regularly charms others and keeps those around them in a good mood so that nobody will understand that they are avoiding work. Blue people are not especially charming. They don't see any need to win anyone over, and they themselves are rather hard to charm. Sweet talk does nothing for them.

Psychopaths have grandiose self-images, placing themselves at the center of everything, and taking credit for other people's ideas. A Blue person will often point out their own mistakes and shortcomings, since nothing is ever good enough—not even them.

Of course, a Blue person may have tried to get you to change your opinion, persuade you to take responsibility for a particular task, and so on, but that happens very openly. The biggest danger is that they bore you to death with the details. It's virtually impossible to be deceived by pure Blue behavior. Irritated, yes definitely. Deceived? Extremely unlikely.

An Important Point

Elsewhere in this book, I describe a manipulation technique called "gaslighting." It means that you convince someone to distrust their own sanity by constantly twisting things around and changing the rules of the game. Blue people never do this; they stick to the plan regardless of what happens around them. But since most of the rest of us are slightly lacking in discipline, we don't have that control. So when we sometimes chance it and cut a corner because we haven't read all the instructions, the Blue leaves us stumped with bewildering questions. *Why didn't you do this or that?*

This can be confusing because it feels as if new rules are being made up in a game we thought we understood. A psychopath does precisely that. They add or subtract from the truth to make you confused and uncertain. It gives them power over you, and in the end you don't know whether you're coming or going.

The Blue person can have a similar effect, even though they are doing the opposite. They point out requirements and steps that have been in the directions the whole time. But since you don't really know what's in the manual, it can feel as if you'll never satisfy them. And then you might well think that they're a psychopath after all.

What Are Our Conclusions?

Blue behavior should not be mistaken for psychopathy because Blue people do what they say they are going to do. They are consistent, which is the opposite of a psychopath's behavior. Your Blue friend is completely knowledgeable on a topic and knows a subject backward and forward, while the psychopath just reads a little bit so that they can pretend to be knowledgeable.

A Recommendation in General

To those who have strong elements of Blue in their profiles, I would like to say the following: The best thing you can do to avoid being mistaken for a psychopath is to show a little more interest in other people and their feelings. You see, a lot of people think that psychopaths are just as calm and cool as Blues are often perceived to be. This is, of course, a misunderstanding, but why not play safe? You could occasionally ask how people feel. And show interest in the answer. It costs almost nothing. Just a moment or two of your (undoubtedly well-managed and valuable) time.

11

How a Psychopath Manipulates a Red Person

The people who would like to manipulate and use you won't tell you your blind spots. They may plan to continue using them to their advantage.

—Assegid Habtewold

Now we'll flip the script. Imagine a boxer who goes into the ring against Mike Tyson. The boxer (unidentified) cannot raise his left arm. Mike Tyson KNOWS about this, but the boxer himself does NOT. Now imagine that Mike Tyson has just been told about the arm. I know, this sounds ridiculous, but stay with me here.

We all have our faults and shortcomings, and a skillful manipulator aims straight at these. Just like a boxer hits you where he guesses it will do the most damage, a psychopath aims for your weakest points. Why? For the same reason the boxer does it: He wants you down on your knees, so he can finish you off.

Let's look at how each color most easily falls into the trap. Soon you will realize why I've harped so much on the value of self-awareness. Your greatest strength is to know yourself. You need to know how your arms work. Both of them.

We will start with the toughest of them all: the Reds.

Taking Down a Red

It might sound odd to say that a Red person can be manipulated. The Reds are strong and powerful and don't let anyone mess with them. They retaliate straightaway, which should make them invincible. They're tough, hard, competitive people who like a fight. How could anyone take them on?

One of the major obstacles to dealing with a Red person is that you must be resistant to a lot of yelling and fighting. So people who are afraid of conflict are not going to get anywhere. On the whole, it is only other people with Red elements who can put up with the fighting.

No, all Reds are not endlessly quarreling with everyone around them, but if you are going succeed in getting a Red to agree with something against their will, conflict will arise. It's part of the pattern. Other Red people can deal with it, because they too don't take anything personally.

And so can psychopaths.

Think about yourself. When somebody scolds you, especially a person you care about, it will affect you negatively. It doesn't feel good at all. You feel uncomfortable, perhaps with a twist of anxiety in your stomach or your chest, when you are criticized or see an angry face.

But how does a psychopath react? Answer: They don't. The psychopath hardly cares. They feel nothing. They see the furious expression and aggressive stance and hear the angry words. But they're not affected. And they wonder how they can make use of that aggressiveness. By getting Reds to direct the anger in another direction, psychopaths can use it to their own advantage.

The Red's Blind Spots

Arrogant, aggressive, walks over people, poor listener, in too much of a hurry, orders people about, controlling, intolerant, and egoistical.

We can find examples in any schoolyard.

Boy A, small in stature but very cunning, who is often beaten up by boy B, goes to the school's worst troublemaker, C, known for his touchiness and short temper. A informs C that B has said some rather offensive things about him. C loses his temper and immediately goes and beats up B. Now A has got his revenge on B without lifting a hand. He has made perfect use of C's aggressiveness. Afterward, he can of course always go to B and say what a shame that he got beaten up; C is such a jerk.

A banal example, perhaps, but the same psychology can be used in more complex situations. If you have some senior staff, one of whom is notorious for his vindictiveness, then you have a perfect situation for manipulation. If you can harness his aggressive manner so that he, for example, attacks your worst competitor, then you have a great resource. The trick is to make sure that you don't get caught in the crossfire.

And while we're talking about being in the line of fire: Imagine that A, B, and C each lead a country with massive military power.

Another angle a psychopath can leverage with Reds is to play on their guilty conscience. (Yes, Red people have one, even though you might not think so.) Or they can confront the Red in a new way. Reds are often surrounded by people who avoid their gaze and scuttle by in the hallway. But think what might happen if they encountered somebody who doesn't do that at all. Who meets them eye to eye. What would happen then?

Let's look at an example.

The Case of Mike and Pernilla

Mike works at a media conglomerate where the wheels have started to roll extremely fast since a new boss has come in. Mike appreciates not having to do any real work. He enjoys the high salary but prefers to let others do the actual work. He is happy to attend important meetings where he can inflate himself and tell everybody what an asset he is for the organization. Several of Mike's colleagues have noticed a pattern fairly quickly. He takes the credit for other people's work, and he always sneaks away when bad news is on the way.

But his new boss still hasn't seen through him. His boss is Pernilla, the new CEO in the company. Mike has observed Pernilla a while and noticed that she is enormously dominant, is quick to flare up, and is not afraid of scolding people in public. She interrupts meetings, strides right in, and just takes over. She demands information from others on very short notice. Pernilla has no problem shouting in the corridor. She seems to be totally insensitive to other people's reactions. The company's owners have given her the task of cleaning up the organization and creating stability and profitability. Within twelve months, and without visibly batting an eyelid, Pernilla has fired a third of the staff and brought in new people that she has recruited herself. She has firm control of every little thing.

Mike is still not doing any real work. Instead, he eats expensive lunches on the company's dime and goes to meetings with important customers. After the meetings, he just hands off the follow-up to someone else. But with the new style of the company, he won't be able to get away with his little game for much longer.

Before Pernilla came into the company, Mike treated all his coworkers a little differently. He had a natural sense for the weaknesses of each and every one. He used to go to one of the senior managers and have a good cry because he was under such pressure, which led that particular manager to take over some of Mike's responsibilities. Mike would always smile at another manager and often grabbed him coffee. This made him look like a really nice guy, which this manager appreciated. The result was that Mike had a strong defender every time the issue of his nonproductivity cropped up.

Mike understood that Pernilla wouldn't fall for any of that. She would be suspicious if he brought her coffee. Ingratiation doesn't work on Red behavior. If Mike were to say that he had a lot to do, Pernilla would simply reply that we all have a lot of work and you'll have to work harder. He would have to use another tactic with her.

Mike realized that the new CEO would be a hard nut to crack. But he wasn't prepared to lose his comfortable position. He had been with the company for many years, and he had it far too good to want to change. So he needed to think up a way to keep Pernilla away from his territory. After studying her from the sidelines, he had some ideas. She seemed to be completely insensitive to what people thought about her extremely tough style. His solution was as brilliant as it was simple. Instead of backing away and keeping his distance from Pernilla like so many of his colleagues, he would get closer.

He demands to report directly to her, although there actually is at least one management level between them. Mike has realized that Pernilla has what is called a "helicopter view." She sees the general outline of things and the big picture, but that makes it hard for her to see what's right next to her. She misses important details. So he positions himself very, very close to her. That way, he can keep track of her and have advance warning if she notices something is off.

Pernilla has a very sharp mind and wants reports from Mike, too. She has no reason to distrust him yet, and he does a good job telling her what she wants to hear. He uses words such as "results," "fast pace," "determination," and "bottom line," because he knows what she values. He lets her know that he admires her ability to act, even when the decision is not popular. This comes dangerously close to flattery, which doesn't work on Pernilla. She is immune to it and would immediately become suspicious if he started inflating her ego with compliments.

But Mike is smarter than that. He says that he would like to be more rational, more focused on the goal instead of getting caught up in emotional things. More like . . . Pernilla. Then he leaves it at that. He doesn't expect any praise. Now he has given her the idea that he respects, perhaps even admires, her.

Why does he do that? Why take that risk? Psychopaths have an intuitive sense for what people need. And even very tough Red people need allies. Although they make controversial decisions, they aren't completely insensitive or inhuman. They can be pragmatic and they do their job, even if it means they sleep badly. But now Pernilla has suddenly found someone who shows appreciation for her sometimes-brusque manner. Unlike virtually all the rest of the staff, Mike doesn't seem scared of her (and he isn't, either—psychopaths are not afraid of anything). And Pernilla can respect that.

Mike does more of the same. He tells Pernilla, "You might not like me saying this, but I'm really impressed by the way you've got this ship back on an even keel." Once again, this isn't direct flattery. And by including a qualification ("you might not like me saying this"), which shows that he knows that he may have stepped a bit out of bounds, he avoids her anger. Instead, he hides behind a mask of honesty that not even Pernilla is immune to. And pretty soon Pernilla has lowered her guard without realizing it. She counts him as one of her allies and doesn't think she needs to keep an eye on him.

How did this happen?

Attempting to manipulate a Red person demands courage. Only somebody who is prepared to take considerable risks would dare to try it. In some cases, it would be utter foolishness. Especially if you're dealing with a senior boss with the power to sack you whenever they feel like it.

Oops, now we're thinking logically again. We decided we weren't going to do that. Yet again, psychopaths don't feel the same way we do. To go in to see a senior boss who is renowned for hating suck-ups and openly flatter said person would give both you and me anxiety. It would be like entering the lion's den and trying to pat the hungry beast. Nobody would do that without very good reason.

For the psychopath, however, this is just a game. And the game doesn't feel the slightest bit stressful for him. He doesn't consider this a risk. If he were exposed, he would just shrug his shoulders and set about negotiating a nice severance package. This is what Red people need to understand. They can be completely tricked by somebody who doesn't see the danger as a danger. Psychopaths radiate self-confidence. And Reds notice and respect confident people. They can even feel admiration for them. At last, somebody on their level.

Although the Red might realize that they, for example, have been flattered, they might still feel a certain respect for the person who had the nerve to do it. And if there is anything Reds respect, it's courage and self-confidence.

It's often effective to praise a Red—subtly, remember that—for something for which they are often criticized. For example, a lot of Reds have heard that they are unfeeling and cold. They think they've just done what needed to be done or said what needed to be said. I have frequently said that if a Red finds out that people don't like them, they can put up with that. But putting up with something isn't the same thing as liking it. Some Reds think that fear is an inevitable part of the job, but, just like everybody else, even Reds would prefer to be liked and respected for the people they are. They just don't show it in the same way as others. So it can be an effective tool to show admiration for them.

Another Trick

You can also defuse a Red's bad behavior. If I know that things are going to erupt with my Red boss and I don't want to deal with it this week, then I can forestall this by making use of a classic manipulation technique called the guilt trip. Because even Reds have a conscience.

Let's have a look at how things are going for Mike.

Mike and Pernilla Again

Sometimes even Mike shows his true colors to Pernilla. He knows he will have to give her some bad news since a project he was leading has completely tanked. He needs something to prevent her from losing her temper and yelling at him when she learns the news. We know he has gained her confidence as somebody who "says it like it is." Even though she's a Red and doesn't reveal anything outwardly, she does have feelings.

This is Mike's first test. He starts by saying, "Now you're going to be angry about this." Pernilla has begun to like Mike, and she doesn't want to hurt him deliberately. So she restrains herself and does all she can not to lose her temper. The news about the project is bad, really bad, but Mike knows how it can be sorted out. He goes so far as to describe the kind of skills that would be necessary to clean up the mess. And naturally he describes Pernilla's strengths.

She takes this as confirmation of her own abilities and takes on the job of cleaning up after Mike. And Mike, in an almost miraculous sleight of hand, has succeeded in delegating a nasty mess to his boss's boss, a person who by now has acquired the in-house nickname "Hatchet Woman." And since Mike has managed to escape a brutal rant, he'll do the same thing again. Now he knows that Pernilla can keep her temper when she wants to. While Pernilla dives into the task of cleaning up the mess, Mike has a long lunch at the golf club. The company pays, of course.

Pernilla is perfectly well aware that she is perceived to be overbearing, and even though she doesn't let it show, it does trouble her a bit. She wants to do a good job, and she does everything within her power to bring the company's owners good results. She's actually pleased with herself for having managed to avoid erupting at Mike. In fact, she feels a degree of gratitude toward him for having helped her remain calm. And Mike has now tightened his grip on her a little more.

Mike continues to sneak in small compliments, but he never does it openly. For example, he makes sure that he makes positive comments about Pernilla to the other members of the senior management that he knows Pernilla listens to. This includes mentioning to the group's head of finance that he is impressed by her big-picture view of the company. The head of finance is Blue and honest, and he will pass this on to Pernilla. Do you know what Mike said? This is an extremely smart move, because it doesn't make Mike look like a sycophant. On the contrary, he didn't tell Pernilla directly because he knew she doesn't like flattery.

Mike still doesn't do any work worth mentioning. He glides around, gets a high salary, and drives a fancy car the company has leased, which he tells his family he bought himself. All his neighbors think it's his car. That suits him because he likes status.

On one occasion, a major customer gets in touch and claims that nothing has been delivered like it should have. Mike manages to take the call, and he is forced to do something. The customer is completely correct. Mike hasn't lifted a finger to help, because that would have meant lots of work, work he had no intention of doing. So he goes in to see Pernilla and says with crumpled-up body language that she is probably going to fire him for this, because now things have gone totally wrong.

Pernilla, who has now (without even realizing it) become accustomed to Mike's guilt-trip tactics, is aware of how many people she has replaced in the company. And she decides there and then that she won't fire Mike regardless of what he is going to tell her. He even manages to elicit a promise from her not to fire him. Then he finally delivers the news that is absolutely catastrophic from beginning to end. And, of course, he has a proposed solution in his back pocket.

And the circus can go on and on.

What Can We Learn?

The trick with Red people is that nothing can be done too openly, and skillful manipulators know that. They never go to the heart of the matter, hiding their actions behind something else. A Red person would immediately confront you if you tried anything silly.

The psychopath's method is often to do something totally unexpected. They can even succeed with Red people through sheer audacity. Once they've gained the confidence of the Red, the boss will simply listen and nod and agree. They won't check up on anything because details are boring, and Reds don't like to look back. The trick is to get under the Red's skin. But as I mentioned earlier, the psychopath doesn't get palpitations from telling lies to their boss's boss. They don't get pink in the face or show any other stress symptom. They don't feel stressed at all. (It isn't any harder than calling for a taxi. What's the worst that can happen?)

Nor do Red persons ask for help. If they should start to feel that something isn't like it should be, they will try to solve it themselves because they have a bit of the lone wolf in them. This is really good news for a master manipulator, who can ply their victim with more of the same medicine for an extremely long time before the Red actually gets help from somebody else.

How long did Mike survive in Pernilla's shadow? Well, the example is based on a real-life situation, and to the best of my knowledge he hung on for almost ten years in that company. When Pernilla did finally expose him, my colleagues and I had to spend six months helping his coworkers deal with the events. The chaos in Mike's wake was so widespread that it was almost impossible to take in, and when things were at their worst, nobody trusted anybody else.

12

How a Psychopath Manipulates a Yellow Person

"Why am I letting you comfort me?" He stared over her head.
"Because I've made sure you have no one else to turn to."

—Kresley Cole, *Lothaire*

The Yellow's weakness is that they refuse to talk about their weaknesses. It's so dreadfully depressing and they think that people in general focus far too much on negative things. Shouldn't we be happy and positive instead? It can definitely be a strength to see the bright side of life, but if you see a pile of trash, then you ought to be able to handle it for what it is.

The Yellow is a typical relationship person. They like to socialize almost constantly and with many different persons. This is extremely enjoyable for them because they get energy from other people. They also give a lot of energy back. They want to have fun, to laugh and fool around. The downside of this is that they are often dependent on others to function well. Without lots of people to interact with, they shrink into themselves and become smaller than they really are. They don't get any stimulation, and their ideas and enthusiasm dry up. Nothing is fun anymore. They don't get to talk, to fool around, and to laugh with others, and they can no longer bounce ideas off the people around them.

They are decidedly social. And that is the downfall of the Yellow. Not having someone to talk to is the worst thing that could happen to them. Since a Yellow person must talk, they need somebody who listens. A clever psychopath who aspires to control a Yellow person will start the manipulation process by separating their victim from other people. The psychopath isolates the Yellow from friends and family and from taking part in social activities. Bit by bit, they cut away their Yellow victim's network of contacts, gradually pulling the person closer to them.

What the psychopath gains from this is obvious: If the victim doesn't have anybody to talk to, the psychopath can then take on the role of being the only person who listens. They become the only person who actually cares, who still appreciates the Yellow despite their faults and shortcomings. (You can be sure that the psychopath has informed the Yellow about these.) The psychopath will play the role of the last remaining confidant and friend, which will make the psychopath incredibly important to the victim. What if the psychopath were to abandon them, too? Then they wouldn't have anybody at all!

But how does a psychopath manage to do this? It's disastrously simple. By turning the Yellow's weaknesses against them. And what does the list of the weaknesses of the Yellow look like? Let's have a look.

Weaknesses of the Yellow Person

Selfish, superficial, egocentric, exaggeratedly self-assured, promises a lot but doesn't deliver, scattered, careless, forgetful, easily offended, sensitive, disorganized, silly, talks too much and for too long, a hopeless listener.

The list could go on, though of course not all of these apply to every Yellow person. If we were to confront a Yellow person with this list, they would be genuinely angry. Or perhaps even sad. And that gives us an important key—the rest of us are unwilling to deliberately make another person sad. We don't want to hurt them; we don't want to get on their bad side.

A psychopath, yet again, doesn't care about the feelings of other people. However bad it makes the Yellow feel to be reminded of these weaknesses, it doesn't matter. The psychopath is going to get what they want, regardless of the price. If their Yellow friend or partner has to cry themselves to sleep . . . well, that's life.

The deceptive and manipulative psychopath often tells the Yellow victim that a friend has said something cruel about them. What a stab in the back! Then things are under way.

Let me give you an example:

The Case of Lars and Anna

Lars is a jolly and positive guy, and he likes talking to everybody. He is open and has a happy nature. Everyone seems to like him, and even if he might sometimes be a bit self-centered, he gets along with most people. He starts dating psychopath Anna, who reads him fairly quickly. And, of course, he isn't very hard to understand. He is open about everything—a bit too open, perhaps. Anna mirrors Lars and gets him to feel comfortable with her. She jokes and laughs and is just wild enough for him to think she's exciting.

For one reason or another, Anna wants to have Lars all to herself, so she can then have full control of him. We needn't worry about the real reason for the time being. But Lars knows so many people. He seems to know everybody! She has to start somewhere.

Anna confides to Lars that Simon, Lars's best friend, has said that he is beginning to get tired of Lars and the way he always exaggerates. Lars is aware of the fact that he does exactly that: He lays it on a bit too thick and tends to exaggerate so that things look better than they really are. This isn't something he does to irritate anybody; it just happens. Even though there is nothing malevolent about Lars, he can easily believe that Simon is annoyed by this behavior.

Anna assures Lars that it wasn't anything serious. The following week, however, Anna tells Lars that Simon now thinks he is arrogant and dominates too many social interactions. Lars begins to feel sad, not only because he is extremely sensitive to criticism, which is something that Anna had realized at an early stage, but also because criticism is even harder to take from such a good friend. It feels like being stabbed in the back.

In the end, Lars thinks it over. It seems rather odd. Would Simon really have said that? But he doesn't have any reason to doubt Anna, who mentions a few other things that Simon has said, all of which seem credible.

Now Lars is seriously worried. He decides to talk with Simon and sort it out, but Anna stops him. He doesn't want to cause a fight, does he? This is something else that she understood about Lars early on: He doesn't like conflict. Instead, she suggests that they should take a short break from Simon, give him some space to get over it. Simon's been in a bit of a funk lately—so dreadfully negative. She doesn't understand what's happened with him. Perhaps he's just going through a rough patch at the moment? Better to leave him be for a while, and he'll come around in the end, don't you think? Lars agrees with her; it sounds reasonable. He's rather pleased that somebody can still think rationally.

Soon Anna has maneuvered Simon completely out of the picture, and she has done it so that it looks as if it's Simon's own choice, when in fact she's behind it all. This is a process that takes time, but Anna has all the time in the world to get Simon away from Lars.

While this is going on, she keeps Lars busy with other things. But he is suffering. It's hard to lose Simon as a friend. They've known each other for many years, and Simon was his very best friend. When he raises the issue with Anna and explains that he's going to contact Simon after all—they've already texted and arranged to get lunch— she finds a way to prevent them from meeting. She doesn't want Lars and Simon to sort out anything at all.

The same day that Lars is going to that lunch with Simon, Anna will either have an angry outburst at home and claim that Lars doesn't love her any longer, or there will be a crisis at her job, or she will suddenly have a serious health scare. Maybe even a close relative who has died. Regardless of why, Lars has to stay at home to support her. He doesn't go to any lunch since he is a kindhearted man who loves his girlfriend. Their next attempt to meet up ends the same way. Without his noticing it, soon a whole year has passed and he hasn't talked with Simon.

Oops! How Did That Happen?

There's no doubt that the Yellow is especially sensitive when it comes to losing their relationships. This creates stress and puts them off-balance. And one way of keeping them off-balance is to sow tiny, tiny seeds of doubt in their minds. Comments like "Do you really have to talk about yourself all the time?" lead to confusion in the Yellow's mind. Sure, it's true, a degree of self-centeredness is often part of Yellow behavior, but even Yellows have to be able to talk about themselves now and then. But the psychopath makes sure that every time they do, they feel guilty. The psychopath will go on and on about the narcissistic attitude of the Yellows person and how it hurts their feelings. Yellows don't want to hurt someone they care about, so they avoid talking about themselves. Fairly soon, they stop dreaming and being creative, and they are on the path to catastrophe.

There are more buttons to press. The psychopath can also claim that the Yellow makes them repeat themselves all the time. When the Yellow person doesn't recall what they're referring to, the answer is, "But you never listen." This, too, is fairly true. "Yellow" is not synonymous with "good listener." And the Yellow person actually knows this. The trouble is, they have so much to say that they sort of forget to listen to what others say.

It's one thing to explain to a Yellow person that they are irritating others and hurting their feelings when they don't listen to others and to therefore ask them to let others into the conversation a bit more often. This is gentle feedback, hopefully packaged in a kind way, so that they have a chance to digest and change their behavior. But it's quite another thing to be forever complaining that they don't listen and to make up things that have never been said. That is psychologically negative manipulation. The persevering psychopath can achieve what others have failed to: They can get the Yellow person, whether a boyfriend or girlfriend, colleague or boss, to listen. And that's what a psychopath does if they want something specific.

There are several ways of breaking down the Yellows: Repeatedly say that they ought to be more serious, shouldn't laugh so much, and shouldn't fool around all the time. They should take life more seriously. The psychopath can pretend to be personally offended by virtually all the jokes that the Yellow makes. Racist, or anti-women, or anti-men, or insensitive, or crude—everything can be criticized. *How could you make a joke about blond people? Did you really make light of that poor dog running into a tree just now? How could you? It was horribly tone deaf; didn't you see how people reacted?* And their humor, which is so central to the Yellow's character, is broken down and withers away. They will become unrecognizable, and more and more people will distance themselves. The formerly vivacious Yellow will be cautious, jumpy, and anxious, always worried about every word that comes out of their mouth.

How Do Things Go for Lars and Anna?

After eighteen months with Anna, Lars is no longer himself. Simon is totally out of the picture and, along with him, so is an entire circle of friends that Lars deeply misses. They have turned their backs on him. They don't like him any longer. Since he has become painfully aware of what a bad person he is, it's so hard to find new friends. Before Anna, he actually had no idea that others thought he was a narcissist on a perpetual ego trip.

Every time he and Anna are at a dinner or a party, she tells him afterward what mistakes he made during the evening. He interrupted Jan or Jan's wife, he told an unsuitable joke to Hank, and he talked far too long with Mia. Perhaps he really did talk too long with Mia, but that was because Mia didn't know who he was, and he wanted to have the chance to talk with somebody who didn't know he was a jerk. It was such a relief to have somebody to talk to, and she laughed the whole evening at his silly tricks.

Anna, who is well aware of what a good time Lars had, wants him to have a bad memory of the evening. So once they're home, she makes a scene and accuses him of having openly flirted with Mia. Anna is in tears and is shouting, and when Lars accuses her of being jealous without any reason, she says that she loves him so much and is terrified of losing him. Can he please, please promise never to speak to Mia again? The whole thing makes Lars feel so guilty that he agrees to this totally crazy promise.

The entire jealousy scene is, of course, fake—a psychopath doesn't feel jealousy. That would imply that Anna actually cares about Lars, but that isn't what this is about. It's about control. (It's actually quite likely that Anna is unfaithful. Like I've said before, psychopaths are often promiscuous, and Anna is probably no exception. Lars, on the other hand, is so inattentive to details that even if Anna were to come home with another man trailing after her, he wouldn't notice.)

After several months of these performances, Lars can hardly face the idea of going out anymore. He prefers to stay home. He sits quietly and watches TV on the weekends, but not football because Anna doesn't like football. She would rather watch old black-and-white films, which he thinks are painfully boring, but that's the only time she wants to sit close to him on the sofa. And now Lars is so hungry for human contact that even though he is extremely unhappy with Anna, he is prepared to do anything to satisfy her. She is all he has nowadays.

What Can We Learn?

Isolation. *Stop fooling around. Stop being so childish. Give me more attention, more, more, more! Otherwise, I'll leave you.* And the Yellow person is caught in the psychopath's net.

Let me emphasize that there are many partners who try to push away the other partner's old circle of friends. The purpose is often to have control, and jealousy is quite often involved. This is never okay. I can't repeat this often enough: If somebody tries to control you, you ought to take a step back and ask yourself why he or she is behaving like that. You ought to immediately question the type of influence. And, obviously, not all the people who use these methods are psychopaths. Sometimes they are simply jealous. But you still need to question how and why they are influencing you.

It's important to remember that even though psychopaths don't feel jealousy any more than they feel sorrow, they can *pretend* to be jealous. They have learned to say things like "you don't love me any longer; I saw that you looked at that guy, and he is much better looking than me." But, in fact, all they want is control.

In the example with Lars, we saw how Anna isolated him bit by bit. The question one could ask now is: If Lars is no longer his bright sunshiny self and won't leave the house, won't that be fairly boring for Anna, too? No, not at all. The thing is that Anna goes wherever she wants and does whatever she feels like doing. And if Lars were to complain that she is having a good time while he sits there at home, she has a ready answer to that, too. Doesn't he want her to enjoy herself? How selfish can you be?

Even though the above example is imaginary, it is an accurate description of how a practiced psychopath would go about things.

13

How a Psychopath Manipulates a Green Person

The rules are simple: They lie to us, we know they're lying, they know we know they're lying, but they keep lying to us, and we keep pretending to believe them.

—Elena Gorokhova

The Green's weakness is that they are afraid of conflict. Conflict is unpleasant, but it seems to lie around every corner. Only troublemakers enjoy conflict. It can be difficult for a Green to say what they really think. For example, they might not like their friend's new sweater at all, but lavish praise on their friend's good sense of style. They've never seen such an elegant sweater. This turns into a problem, of course, when the friend offers to lend it to them.

The Green person is afraid of change as well; they don't like new plans. They don't want to be the center of attention or to be criticized in public. Neither do they like talking to large groups (meaning more than five people) unless they know its members well. The Green is an introvert and something of an observer. Sometimes it can be very hard to get any real answers from them, even to direct questions. Hearing a yes when the Green means no is extremely common.

Which of these weaknesses is the Green person aware of? Naturally, this varies from person to person, but a description along the lines of "unwilling to change" is probably most common. *You never want to mix anything up; you just sit there. Can't we move, redecorate, change something?* No, things are just fine like they are!

Weaknesses of the Green Person

Afraid of conflict, long-winded, unwilling to change, stubborn, sulky, reserved, cowardly, passive, sneaks away, doesn't take responsibility, dishonest, oversensitive to criticism, and indecisive.

If a psychopath wants to get to a Green person, they tend to direct their attack toward the Green's sensitivity to criticism and fear of conflict. There are essentially two primary ways to reach a Green person. Which of these two methods is most effective will depend on whether the context is work or personal, like a friendship or romantic relationship.

Let's look at a personal relationship. The Green woman is quite often aware that she lacks initiative. Together with a similarly Green man she will easily find herself just sitting there on the sofa while her dreams and plans for the future remain dreams and plans. If neither of them gets to work, the job won't get done. Which leads us—paradoxically—to Red behavior. It is not impossible that a Green person will be impressed by the ability of their opposite (the Red) to take action. The Red has a powerful personality and acts decisively in every situation. There is always something happening, and a Red person in a good mood can get an unbelievable number of things done in a very short time. Building a fence or painting a garage hardly takes any time at all.

This is a simplified example, but it illustrates the principle. The way to reach a Green *might be* to act Red. Show that you're someone they can rely on when the going gets rough. And since Green people are happy not having to shoulder the heavy responsibility of making decisions that can have long-term implications, they will happily hand over that power to someone else.

Once the psychopath has won the Green's confidence and gotten close to them, the manipulation can begin.

The following example is, unfortunately, 95 percent based on real life.

The Case of Katie and Ed

Katie is a gentle, friendly divorced woman. She has three children, all under ten years old, and she has been single for just over a year. It's not a life she likes. On the contrary, she thinks that kids should have two parents. But she hasn't met the right man since her divorce. The men she's dated have either been too much like her—that is, rather passive—or they have been in too much of a hurry to try to get her into bed.

Then she meets Ed. He is distantly acquainted with Katie's friend Kristina. They meet by chance at a block party in the neighborhood, and Ed soon has his eye on Katie. He doesn't do anything at first, but spends half an hour studying her: how she behaves, whom she talks to, what she seems to laugh at. Then he goes up to her and introduces himself. He's friendly, but dominant at the same time. He fetches her a drink, suggests what she should eat from the barbecue, and generally takes the initiative. But he doesn't make any attempt to flirt with her. This surprises her, since she is very attractive and all the men who know that she's single inevitably flirt with her.

Ed has more complex plans than that. He has noticed Katie's shy manner and realizes that she needs time to get accustomed to him. So he leaves the party without saying goodbye. He does, however, turn up three days later at her local supermarket. What a coincidence! They chat, and he does his shopping quickly and efficiently while Katie wanders among the shelves. Now she's rather impressed by how efficient and decisive he is. If only she could be more like that! He leaves the shop as quickly as he arrived. After repeating this interaction several times, he invites her out for dinner, they end up in bed, and within a week he's moved in with her.

We still don't know what his goal is. But if he wants to hold on to somebody as long as possible, there's no better person to target than a Green. She will want to help him, to support a fellow human being, because that's one of the Green's greatest strengths. He might say that he has an apartment just outside town and that it's a rather long drive. They might as well meet at her place every time. Bit by bit, he moves in. While Katie is totally overwhelmed by his energy, she lets him do what he wants in her house. He moves her favorite furniture, fills the fridge with food he likes, pushes her clothes to one side in the closet. And he parks an unusually flashy car in the driveway. A car that he, for some reason, never seems to use.

Ed's way of controlling Katie is totally different from how, for example, Anna controlled Lars. From the start, Katie is not somebody who goes out every evening. She doesn't invite lots of friends over when the children are spending the weekend with their father. No, her style is to devote all her spare time and attention to her partner. This is something that Ed immediately makes use of. He lets her do the shopping, wash his clothes, iron his shirts, clean the house, make the food—all the things that Ed doesn't feel like doing. In doing this, he gets Katie to feel important and valuable in his eyes.

It's not long before he has a problem with his paycheck. The accounts department has gotten some of the figures wrong: Can he borrow a few hundred bucks until the idiots at the office have sorted out the mess?

If she says yes, he has broken through a barrier. He only asks her for a small loan. He wouldn't ask for thousands the first time, but just a few hundred is safe. And naturally Katie goes along with this. Ed is such a reliable guy. Of course he will pay her back. But paying back the loan is not in Ed's plans at all. He knows that he can exploit Katie's innate kindness. For him, this was a test. Now he knows that she is willing to open her wallet for his sake. So he continues, one step at a time. He has forgotten his wallet almost every time they go to a restaurant, but she has happily gotten hers out instead. He wants to see how far he can go.

And once Katie has started giving him money, she will continue to do so. Because that's how it works. Once she has started helping him, she will help him again. And again.

How to Turn Somebody's Strengths Against Them

When a psychopath chooses a Yellow victim, it's about suppressing their personality, changing the victim's view of themselves so that the psychopath can govern them. But Green people don't have inflated egos. They don't go around thinking they're better than anyone else. They're more likely to suppress themselves and tell anybody who wants to listen about their weaknesses. All the psychopath needs to do is to feed that trait.

Just like the Yellows, Greens are relationship people, and isolation from the rest of the world is a horrific threat for them. All the psychopath needs to do when a Green woman looking in the mirror says that she has put on weight is to agree. *Yes, perhaps you have put on a few pounds.* All men know that the question is dangerous, but for the man who does actually want to tear down his partner, all that is required is to confirm the weight gain. And her self-esteem, which was fragile before, takes another blow.

After she made dinner and asks, "Was the sauce good?" "Well, perhaps it could have had a bit more salt, a bit less butter, and a little more heat to it." Very little is required to keep a Green person anxious over how they are performing. And if she should protest, all he has to do is raise his voice a tiny, tiny bit. The skillful psychopath only needs to sharpen their tone the slightest degree to get the Green to take cover from the potential conflict. Because, as usual, they won't want a fight.

Since Katie cares about her family and how her family looks like from the outside, this too is an effective weapon. If the psychopath wants something—money, time on their own, some sexual favor—all he needs to do is hint that he might leave her. That would be a punishment that she isn't prepared to endure. She has to show that she can keep a man. And the children need a male role model, after all.

How did it end, the drama of Katie and Ed?

After six months, Katie and her children only eat food that Ed approves of. It might be a question of his only wanting chicken or only beef or that he's now a vegetarian. It doesn't matter. The food is always bought by Katie. Unfortunately, Ed has had some difficulties with employment for a while and has no income. He sold his car, and she dared to ask him what happened to the money. This resulted in a fight, during which he pretended to be offended by her questions. Then he got angry, really angry. Ed's fury was so strong that Katie—afraid of conflict—has not said anything to contradict him a single time since then.

Of course, this was all planned by Ed. He knows that she is afraid of fighting. And shouting at her was the best thing he could have done. Now all that's necessary is one angry look and she'll cave in and give him everything he wants. And he makes sure he takes it. Yet again: Ed doesn't care about Katie. She is just a replaceable asset, nothing more.

In this case, it's mostly about money. Ed likes to watch TV. He watches lots of movies online while Katie is at work. This costs hundreds of dollars a month and ends up on her internet bill. Together with Ed's other pleasures, Katie's limited savings have been used up. Ed even resorted to making her empty the children's savings accounts—money that had been put aside years before he came into the picture.

Now Katie is really worried about her finances. One salary isn't very much to provide for a family, especially when Ed squanders her money. Ever since she gave him the PIN to her debit card, he comes home with clothes he has bought, nice clothes that he won't even use.

Katie raises the question of money. She is terrified of his sudden outbursts of rage, but she has no choice. She is broke. Since he is a psychopath, he has never thought about what he would do when the money runs out. So he improvises. Without feeling the slightest shame, he suggests that she go to the bank and borrow some money. Katie is horrified because her mother always told her that you shouldn't get into debt without a very good reason.

But Ed is cunning. He asks her how long she is going to allow her mother to govern her. For goodness' sake, she will soon be forty years old! Isn't it time she freed herself from the chains of her parents and made some financial decisions of her own? He believes in her; he knows she can do it. Here, he builds up her feeble self-confidence and says she is going to manage to do this all on her own. And he will help her, of course. Soon he'll have a job, too. In fact, he has a job interview this week. He hadn't mentioned it before, because it was going to be a surprise.

All of this is completely spontaneous, since Ed makes up stories as easy as breathing. She is overjoyed. A job interview! She gives him a big hug and promises to go to the bank the very next morning. Everything will be sorted out, and they'll soon be back on their feet.

Katie borrows seven thousand dollars on Ed's advice. And when she has the money in her bank account, he immediately asks for half of it. She wonders why—she's the one who handles the household costs. She needs the money for lots of unpaid bills. And it is urgent. But Ed explains that if he has a bit of money in his account, then she won't have to keep giving him cash all the time. Reluctantly, she gives him half of what she has borrowed. He spends it in two days, but he can't explain on what. Naturally, he immediately starts to work on her again to get the rest of the money.

And so it goes on. He persuades her to borrow more money, the amounts higher and higher, until the bank says no—no more money. When Katie is heavily in debt and penniless, Ed will disappear. Perhaps he will simply be gone one day when she comes home from work. Behind him, he will leave a lonely little family on the edge of ruin. Katie will never dare confess to anybody that he has conned her for an entire year.

What Can We Learn?

Does this sound rather exaggerated? Well, it isn't. There are obviously lots of relationships where one partner likes to spend and the other prefers to save. Sometimes one of them has a much higher salary, for example. It's fairly common for there to be a lack of balance between the different individuals' economic circumstances. It is often the man who, whether deserved or not, earns the higher salary. But in a working relationship, both partners use their money jointly and respectfully. They are a family, after all.

Situations where one partner systematically exploits the other to avoid having to pay anything themselves are something totally different. Psychopaths are unusually skilled at getting you to open your wallet. They behave like Ed in the above example. They start small and then see how far they can go. And little by little, they will get a firm grip on your wallet. Leeching off others is a distinctly psychopathic feature. They feel no shame and no remorse for letting others pay.

Some people would never dream of giving money to a person they've just met. They are of no interest to the psychopath, who will just jump over to the next victim. Because there are always new victims.

14

How a Psychopath Manipulates a Blue Person

Whenever you keep score in love, you lose.

—Kamand Kojouri

This is interesting. I would say that of all the colors, Blue people are the hardest to manipulate. The reason is simple: The Blue knows what's going on. They know what you said before and they remember details. They write down what they hear. They keep emails and receipts and know how things work.

By now, you know that a psychopath lies indiscriminately and that when they are exposed for having told lies, they have a new lie to confuse the issue. And, naturally, they would lie to a Blue person, too. But there they meet with a problem. The Blue coworker or boss or friend or partner will quickly expose the lie for what it is. Blues keep track of facts and double-check all sorts of things. (Yes, your Blue boss probably checks what you do without your knowing it. That is just how they are. There is nothing bad about it; they just like keeping tabs on what's going on.)

If a psychopath does want to manipulate a Blue person for their own benefit, they need a special approach. It won't work to yell "This is how it is!" The Blue will check it out and discover it's not like that at all. Rational and task-oriented, they simply go back to the office psychopath and say you were wrong. How can you explain that?

In a relationship, you can't say, "I paid for the holiday; your share was $1500." Your Blue partner/friend will ask to see the receipt. Not necessarily because they don't believe you, but because they simply want to see the receipt. (And if the amount is not exactly right, they won't give you $1,500; they will give you $1,486, because that is exactly 50 percent.)

This means that you can't get away with much with a Blue person. Many psychopaths read up a bit on certain subjects, just enough to make it look like they really know what they're talking about and thus get people to listen. But Blue people don't fall for that. They delve deep into everything. One of their foremost weaknesses is, indeed, that they can't keep from digging deeper into something, figuring out how something really works. Sometimes this irritates those around them, but in this case it's definitely to the Blue's advantage. However, the Blue won't necessarily make a big fuss about the psychopath's dodges. The Blue person doesn't feel any need to share their opinion publicly, but they've made up their own mind. That person at the far end of the corridor can't be relied on.

So are Blues immune to manipulation?

Unfortunately, they are not.

The Blue Person's Irritatingly Small Failings

Evasive, brusque and surly, suspicious, petty, grumbling, dissatisfied, a stickler for details, indecisive, reserved, callous, lacking social skills, slow, etc.

As you see, the Blue, too, has quite a lot of failings. And, as usual, the psychopath ascertains what these weaknesses are. Not all Blues are suspicious of those around them, but they are less relationship-oriented than the Greens and the Yellows. Most people value relationships more than our Blue friends do. Many times, this is the Blue's strength; they don't care if they are perceived as a bit dull. They might even agree: That's just what they're like.

But, like everything else, this can be turned against them.

The Case of George and Roger

George is a person with an extremely systematic way of thinking. He works as a controller in an accounts department in a large company. He has been there a long time and is renowned for never missing anything. His eye for detail is legendary, but he is also seen as a bit standoffish. He rarely, if ever, takes part in social activities such as happy hours or office parties. He simply isn't interested in his colleagues. He knows that he needs them to do his job, but he decides when he'd like to socialize. He is well aware of how he is perceived at the office, but since he has a different social circle in his private life, it doesn't bother him that the others see him as something of a nerd.

The department gets a new boss, Roger, who quickly realizes that George is an odd character. He hears how everyone praises George for his unparalleled experience and competence. Finally, Roger gets tired of this and thinks it would be exciting to see if the legendary George could be brought down to earth. After sitting and talking with George, Roger soon realizes that he will be a hard nut to crack. He tries praising George—without much reaction. George knows his own competence and is immune to praise and to anyone trying to suck up to him. Roger then tries criticizing George for some small detail. But he doesn't fall for that either. Completely calm and seemingly unperturbed, he explains that Roger doesn't know what he is talking about, because we use a different system here. George gives Roger a lecture on the topic, which Roger does not like one little bit. Roger is convinced of his own brilliance and doesn't allow anybody to contradict him. He decides to make a total fool of George.

By observing what George does in the company, Roger soon sees that he—despite his status as a specialist—is a lone wolf. This tells Roger that he can operate behind George's back without his finding out about it.

No sooner said than done. Roger talks to one member of the staff at a time to find out what people actually think of George. He quickly comes to learn that they all respect him but think he is a bit aloof. Roger then puts his plans into action.

He can't find any serious mistakes to pin on George—nobody would be fooled by that. Since he probably can't manipulate George himself, he will try to manipulate all the others in the department. He goes to A and says that he has come to fetch some documents that George has said A will have. But A is perplexed, answering that he gave those to George long ago. Roger shrugs his shoulders and says that it was probably just an oversight—no problem.

Later the same week, he goes to B on a similar errand. Then to C and D. Each time, he is careful not to question George's competence in the slightest, and he makes sure all the errands are about trifles. He has soon established an awareness that George can miss things sometimes. Since this is an accounting department, there is lots of Green and Blue behavior, which means that they don't go to George and confront him. This is something that Roger had realized from the start. He knows that introverted members of staff keep a lot to themselves, and he makes shameless use of that.

Roger continues with his plan and plants one weird rumor after the other about George. He asks one member of staff, F, to come in for a little talk and the subject is whether F has seen anything strange about George recently. F answers that he hasn't seen anything strange— George is just like he usually is. When F asks for an example, Roger shakes his head and says it probably wasn't anything. He soon gets quite a lot of people in the department to start rethinking their impression of the infallible George. And bit by bit, the formerly brilliant halo becomes more and more tarnished.

This Is Going to Take Some Patience

Roger realizes that he must proceed very slowly because no one will believe him if he declares over coffee one morning that George has suddenly become senile. Nobody would buy that, so he needs to proceed with caution. Taking away a Blue person's credibility is one way to destroy other people's faith in them. That can be accomplished by manipulating those around the Blue person into believing they have become careless.

In order to do this, Roger must also build up his own credibility. This is a well-known tactic in politics. You can't make your opponent change their stance on an issue, but by questioning their personal behavior or their morals, you can get people to stop listening to them. We know that there isn't really any connection between the message and the messenger—facts should be facts, after all. But we're influenced by who voices a particular message. Think about it: If you were to meet Hitler and he said, "Earth is not going to survive unless we eliminate our greenhouse gas impact immediately," you might rethink your view of climate change. Because everything he says must have some dark, ulterior motive. And it works the same way in the other direction: If you were to bump into your favorite thinker or writer on a street corner and she claimed that we can completely disregard the greenhouse effect because it's not connected to human behavior, then you might start wondering. Roger understands all this, and so he finds himself some allies.

The researchers Robert Hare and Paul Babiak call these "pawns," resources that can be readily sacrificed and whose function is to act as useful idiots for the psychopath. These allies fall completely for the psychopath's charm and will always consider him the best guy in the world. That is how Roger will build up his credibility as deliverer of the news that George has become inept. Every time somebody criticizes Roger, the pawns will come to his rescue, and the critic will appear to be petty or jealous.

Blue behavior is difficult for most people to handle. Blue people have an uncanny ability to pay attention to their work, and they don't normally make any mistakes. It's far more likely that they'll point out your mistakes. If they can't find any errors in other people's work, perhaps they'll finally start doubting their own abilities. Being socially ostracized is not necessarily a problem for a Blue, but if the Blue person is prevented from doing quality work, their self-confidence will begin to be eroded at the edges. If you can fool them into thinking that they've made real mistakes (even when they haven't), things will really begin to unravel.

Back to George and Roger

After six months, George has been caught in so many little errors that they can't be ignored. Roger has spread lots of malicious rumors, all of which are somewhat plausible. This has led his colleagues to think that George has lost his touch. And, of course, nobody is perfect after all. There could be all sorts of reasons for George's poor performance. Perhaps Roger has spread a rumor that George is having problems at home. That he has confided in his new boss about his divorce and that he doesn't want to talk about it. He wants everyone to treat him the same way. This isn't a major problem, since George is mostly a loner. So nobody discusses it with him.

Roger now believes he has won over the staff, and he has a large number of pawns at his disposal, so he embarks upon phase 2. He moves up all meetings fifteen minutes earlier and informs everyone except George. So George starts to come late with a strange regularity. Everyone notices and thinks this confirms that George is losing his touch. Can't he even read a clock?

Now George goes to Roger and asks why he hadn't been informed about the new meeting time. Roger says that of course he was informed. He shows him an email that he has sent to George. It looks completely real, but Roger has manipulated the mail addresses so that George never received it. Roger now tells George that the staff is losing confidence in him. They say you're beginning to lose your touch. Can you pull yourself together?

George can't understand any of this and asks for concrete examples of his mistakes. Roger doesn't give him any, instead telling him that his coworkers wanted to be anonymous. They didn't want to talk directly with George, and if Roger gives examples, then George will know who has brought forward complaints. That would be a betrayal of confidence, Roger explains. George finds it difficult to object to that logic, as he himself is a rule follower.

Roger tells him that his carelessness is a serious problem. George doesn't respond but goes and sits at his desk. Because he is so introverted and doesn't want to interact with his colleagues unnecessarily, he does nothing, says nothing. He doesn't want to talk with them, and they don't want to talk with him.

To really shake George, Roger now orders him to take part in a staff conference. This is the first time George has spent a night away from home in ten years. This forces him to socialize relatively intimately with the very people who have become convinced that he is failing at his job. The entire weekend conference is just one long nightmare for George. He usually gets asked to present at large conferences like this, but now someone else has been given that job, and he realizes that his status as controller is seriously threatened.

He still doesn't say anything to anybody else, partly because he doesn't usually talk to them, and partly because it's evident to him that those idiots don't understand anything. Roger blames more and more mistakes on George and finally transfers him to another post in the department. After all, you can't have a person in such a critical position if they're so careless. George still insists that he hasn't made any mistakes. Now he spends his evenings and nights double-checking and triple-checking everything he does. He's heading for a breakdown because he wants to clear his name, his good reputation.

George is now given very basic work, far below his level of competence. Dissatisfied and miserable at work, he finally tells his wife what is happening. She thinks he ought to change jobs since the company seems to be completely ungrateful. After all those years he has devoted to the firm, this is the thanks he gets?

Now George is really in a pickle. At the office, they don't seem to trust him. His wife wants him to get a new job. But he liked the job he had. He was comfortable and happy there until a year ago. Now everything has collapsed. He's always in a bad mood at home and at work, which only reinforces the impression that he is difficult to work with. George finally goes to his coworkers and blames it all on Roger, but they're on Roger's side—they are his loyal pawns.

To make a final attempt to sort things out once and for all, George arranges a meeting via email with his boss Roger at ten o'clock on a Monday. He spends the weekend preparing for what is perhaps the most important meeting he has ever had. He must save his own skin. When he comes to the meeting with a folder full of arguments, he's scolded by Roger. He can't just come waltzing in any old time: He should have been here an hour ago. Why is he so late? Doesn't he take anything seriously? George is in shock and goes back to look at his online calendar. And, of course, it says nine o'clock there. How is that possible? He doesn't know that Roger has gone in and changed the time in the invitation sent to George.

The game goes on for another six months, until George is finally made redundant and there is no more work for him to do.

What Can We Learn?

Going after a Blue person is quite a challenge, even for the most cunning psychopath. It would probably be a lot simpler to ensnare a Blue person based on a personal relationship. This is a fairly simple example, but imagine a man in his early forties who still hasn't met the right partner. Then along comes a beautiful woman who promises him her everlasting love. She gives him all her attention and praises all his best features. He's never experienced anything like this before and is an easy mark for the con woman. Since psychopaths also use sex as a weapon, this can end up a real mess.

Even though Blue people are less dependent on relationships than other colors, they do build very close relationships in their private lives, but only a few. And in such situations, their defenses are no stonier than anybody else's.

15

Common Manipulation Techniques

If you are an approval addict, your behavior is as easy to control as that of any other junkie. All a manipulator need do is a simple two-step process: Give you what you crave, and then threaten to take it away. Every drug dealer in the world plays this game.

—Harriet B. Braiker

Personally, I am a great believer in straight talk. There's no point in dancing around the facts when it comes to ways that a psychopath can and will mess up your life. If we're going to see through the smoke screens, we need to understand what allows them to manipulate us and what methods they use. Here are some important examples of just how they do it.

There are lots of manipulation techniques. You could probably fill a whole book with them. Here, however, I have listed the most common techniques and described the different varieties of each of them. There is overlap between many of these techniques, but each focuses on a slightly different way of controlling someone else. Any one on its own might not seem particularly dangerous. But imagine a psychopath who uses two, three, or maybe even all the manipulation techniques at the same time. The consequences would be disastrous.

What's strange—and horrible—is that most psychopaths use similar means to achieve their ends. It seems to be hardwired into their personalities to know how to behave to hurt others. The reports from across the world of how psychopaths manipulate their surroundings can vary in the precise details, but when you look at the actual methods they use, they are horribly similar. Sometimes I wonder if there is a special *modus operandi* of psychopathic techniques being taught somewhere.

Technique 1: Arbitrary Positive Reinforcement

What does that mean? Giving an individual strong reinforcement and praise—and then sometimes withholding it without cause. This makes a person dependent on an unreliable source of affirmation in order to feel good about themselves. This is an extremely effective tactic to get control over another person. By using this technique, the manipulator motivates their victim to do exactly what the manipulator wants them to do in order to receive the reinforcement they are craving.

Imagine a drug addict whose body is screaming for a particular drug. He gets the drug and immediately feels better. But before long, he feels worse again and needs more of the drug. If he gets some, the pattern is repeated; if he doesn't get any, he will soon feel worse and worse. The person who has the drugs has power over the drug addict, which is why addicts would do anything for their next fix. Every dealer in the world knows this.

We all look for confirmation and affirmation of some sort. It's built into our human nature. We are primarily emotionally governed beings, and there are things that make us feel good, just as there are things that make us feel bad.

Arbitrary positive reinforcement works extremely well on people who have weak self-esteem, so if you suspect you fall into that category, read this very carefully. You might be one of those people who need to hear that you've done a good job. You glow hearing your boss say that you've been clever. I must admit that I belong to that category. It isn't that I make a big deal about being praised, and I don't even have a boss. But I most definitely feel good when somebody whose judgment I respect very highly gives me positive feedback. That means that I'm vulnerable to this technique, since there might be a key person whose judgment I really care about.

Human Laboratory Mice

In a scientific test with laboratory mice, they created a black room and a white room. The black room only had one feature: a white door. When a mouse was put inside the black room, it wandered around for a while until it found the white door and entered the white room. Inside the white room was a bit of cheese that the mouse gobbled up. It took the mouse three attempts to improve the time it took to get from the black room to the white room. Each time, it was rewarded with a piece of cheese: positive reinforcement. As long as it got this reward, it was prepared to perform the same behavior.

But we aren't laboratory mice, are we?

Imagine I came from a work environment where praise and positive feedback were very rare. What you usually heard was a long list of all the things you did wrong, and—as we've seen earlier—all of us have our faults, so there is always something to criticize.

A lot of bosses are absolutely hopeless at giving praise. They spend most of their time criticizing, not necessarily because they're trying to be mean: In my experience, it's mainly because they are simply bad managers, and it never occurred to them that praise is important in leadership.

Now I find myself in a new job where I get a warm welcome from my new boss. She immediately notices my abilities and praises me for being quick, energetic, creative, hardworking, and for fifteen other things that I'm secretly proud of. Finally, somebody sees me for the person I am and actually appreciates my efforts. Wow!

How does this influence my behavior? Of course, I'll want to work even harder, faster, more creatively, and so on to get more of that delightful positive feedback. Within just a couple of weeks, the boss had made me feel more comfortable in my job than I've ever felt in my career thus far. And it feels like this for a couple of months.

Now imagine that my new boss becomes oddly silent. Suddenly, I don't get any positive feedback. How will I deal with this change, going from being appreciated because I am an ambitious employee to suddenly hearing only silence? No feedback, no attention—every time I see my boss in the corridor, she looks straight through me as if I don't exist. She doesn't answer questions, and, judging by her expression, it's as if I weren't there at all.

What's my reaction? How would you react? I would immediately feel stressed. What's wrong? I must have made a serious mistake, since she's suddenly ignoring me. What do I do? I should work even harder to get back in her good graces. But for one seemingly never-ending month, I don't hear anything. I start to doubt my own ability. Have I misunderstood? Was she never impressed by my work?

Then, all of a sudden I'm summoned to the boss's office again. She praises me effusively for my work. Struck dumb by gratitude, I stumble out of her office, overjoyed to be appreciated again. I've instantly forgotten that I was miserable right before this meeting. Perhaps I'll even berate myself for having been so sensitive.

I might even silently defend my boss's earlier behavior. She hadn't noticed what good work I'd done, she was under stress, she has so much responsibility—how could she keep track of what everyone is doing? And what's much worse, I might start questioning my own value. Perhaps I'm not quite as sharp as I think. The reason my boss was silent for all those weeks was probably because I wasn't doing good work. It was all my fault.

When you read this, you might think that I simply ought not to be so desperate for attention. Shouldn't I have a little more confidence of my own? Or perhaps I could have asked for feedback from someone else to evaluate how I was doing? Well, yes, if we were logical beings. But now I've become accustomed to praise from the boss herself. And when that disappeared, I became uncertain. I'd lost something and I wanted it back.

Praise is a motivational factor. It encourages me to move forward. But when I lose it, there is emptiness.

Think of how a child functions. They're willing to do almost anything to earn the approval of their parents. They'd rather be shouted at than met with silence, just so they know that Mom and Dad care. Adults function in basically the same way, except on a more complex level. We become dependent on confirmation. It becomes a sort of drug that we find it hard to do without.

SO WHY DID SHE DO IT?

Now if my boss asks me for something that I might not really want to do, I will consider whether doing what she has asked will earn her praise and approval. If I think there is a chance I'll be in her good graces, I'll eagerly do whatever she's asked. When I do it, I bask in her praise again. I feel better, and everything seems fine. Bit by bit, my boss can now get me to do work that isn't my responsibility and take care of tasks I would never have done before. This could be anything from picking up her dry cleaning to doing things that could be decidedly dubious from a legal perspective.

Then, suddenly, my boss flips into silent mode again. Turns up her nose at something I say in a meeting. Completely ignores me, behaves yet again as if I don't exist. Using this tactic, she has me on an emotional roller-coaster ride. Remember that skillful manipulators like to make people feel insecure. It serves their purposes. Perhaps she wants to ask me to do something inappropriate or to get me to work even harder without asking for a raise. And bit by bit, she will change my behavior so that I am always at her beck and call.

(Now imagine that this were to happen in a relationship. The power would lie entirely with the manipulator. To keep someone's love, we're prepared to go very far.)

ARE THERE ANY COUNTERMEASURES?

If you mainly have Red traits, this kind of emotional bait and switch might make you angry. It's a disgraceful way to behave. To hell with the boss. On the whole, you are less dependent on confirmation from others. Besides, you are well aware of what your strengths and abilities are. In your work, you don't need as much affirmation as do others. Obviously, you're not completely unmoved, but you would probably have the courage to question the behavior of your boss if you notice the pattern. If you did, she would deny it right away; then you can decide whether you believe her.

The same would be true if you're primarily Blue. You have your own methods for evaluating the work you do. You're perfectly well aware of the quality of your work. If you are satisfied with your work, that's enough. Besides, you're slightly suspicious of praise. "Buttering-up" has never appealed to you, anyway. That doesn't mean that Red and Blue persons would be completely immune to this very dirty tactic, but it would take longer to build up the uncertainty that I described in the example above. Since the profiles of Reds and Blues are task-oriented, their desire for a good relationship with the boss is not as strong as for the other colors.

If you mainly have Yellow in your profile, there is a strong likelihood that you would suffer deeply from this method. You are naturally dependent on approval—public approval being preferable—and when you receive it, you feel amazing.

Many Yellow people I meet deny having this trait because they know that it can be perceived as self-centered and slightly childish. An adult is expected to do good work without a lot of praise from the boss, right? But I would advise you to be honest with yourself. You know how you are influenced by praise. And you know how you feel when you suddenly find yourself without that praise. Without affirmation from the people whose opinions you value most highly, you're going to feel vulnerable and weak. Face the facts.

A purely Yellow person actively looks for signs of approval in other people's faces. They would like approval from everybody, but Yellows also have their favorites. And if it's the boss, then their opinion will be important. The Yellow person is very sensitive to changes in the relationship with the boss, a fact that this method takes advantage of.

Praise, silence, praise, silence.

The Yellow might talk with their coworkers about it, but since it looks bad not to be praised by the boss, they might not broach the subject. They might keep it to themselves, since they previously boasted about how pleased the new boss was with them.

Nor will the Yellow have the courage to confront the boss about this behavior—particularly if we are talking about a Yellow-Green profile. That could lead to the risk of conflict, and they'll feel uncomfortable and miserable at their workplace. Bit by bit, the Yellow will fall silent.

The Green coworker is also sensitive to relationship problems, but suffers quietly from the beginning. They, too, will never confront their boss about the behavior. That's not an option for them. But the problem is less severe than it would be with a Yellow. This is because of the way the positive reinforcement has been conveyed from the beginning. If the boss had not read the Green properly, they might praise the Green person loudly in front of the entire group at a meeting. That would be wonderful for a Yellow, who wants to be in the spotlight. But for the Green, it's actually a terribly awkward situation. So if the boss stops the public shows of public affirmation, the Green would actually be relieved. But if the boss has realized that the Green prefers to be called into their office and given personal praise behind closed doors, then that is the form of praise that they will take away. And here the Green has an obvious weakness.

Positive reinforcement is a terrible weapon in many cases, which might sound weird. But the trick lies in the fact that the manipulator initially accustoms their victim to a situation with ice cream and balloons and all the nicest praise. When that suddenly disappears, the problems begin. People who have found themselves on the receiving end of this emotional pendulum often end up on long-term sick leave or simply leave their jobs because they can't cope with the mental strain. And the manipulating boss moves on to the next victim until they are surrounded by only yes-men.

Technique 2: Love Bombing

Imagine that the manipulator wants to control a person they're in a close relationship with—their partner, for example. Here it isn't only Yellow and Green people who risk falling into the trap but all colors. And if you've never experienced real love before, you're an easy victim for the manipulator's evil plans.

The expression "love bombing" has been used by psychologists for many years to describe this very insidious tactic. A true psychopath is enormously skillful at using this extremely effective weapon against the person they claim to love more than anyone else.

The psychopath, who can be very attractive and knows how to use that, starts by declaring their true love earnestly and nakedly. An example: A woman is completely candid and tells you during a romantic dinner (that you pay for) that she has never met anyone like you. In all her long life, you're the most incredible person she has ever come across, and she wants to spend the rest of her days with you. She emphasizes all of your positive sides, particularly things you yourself are extremely proud of, and admires your personality. You've never heard such a song of praise—ever.

How can you resist? The answer is that you probably can't. If you're Red, you are always hearing about how you can be a little insensitive. Now along comes somebody who doesn't seem to have the slightest problem with that. If you're Yellow, you've been told that you talk too much and take up too much space. Now you've met a soul mate who wants nothing more than to listen to yet another funny story. And the way she laughs! To the Green, she'll say that she loves the strong, silent type who can give her stability and security. And the Blue, who has always worried that they were a bit conventional and boring, now gets to hear that their well-ordered intellect is incredibly sexy.

I know—when you look at it from the outside, it sounds almost too simple. But imagine what it would mean for you to hear that you are the most fantastic person ever to walk the earth, and to hear that from somebody you feel strongly for. You are showered with small presents, flowers, friendly gestures, warmth, kisses, and admiration from morning to evening. We're talking about emotions now, so skip the logic. You won't be able to resist.

The problem is that the psychopath is only preparing you for the unavoidable blow. One beautiful day, it might be after six months or a year—it depends on how long-term this plan is, and also possibly on your ability to foot the bills—the love bombing suddenly ceases. Now, perhaps, you've already moved in together or even gotten married. All you can do is follow along. You haven't a chance.

An Escalating Process

One beautiful day, she doesn't reply to the text message you sent that morning. There's no phone call at noon when you're both having your lunch. The hand that usually holds yours when you go for a walk now stays in her pocket. Perhaps your darling suddenly starts smiling at another person in a way that doesn't feel good at all, though she would deny it if you said anything. For a whole week, there's no sex, which has never happened before. And suddenly she begins criticizing you for parts of your personality that she has previously praised.

If you're Red, you'll now suddenly hear that you always demand to get your own way and that you smother her by wanting to decide everything. A Yellow person will be charged with being far too silly and sloppy and never listening to their beloved. The Green will be accused of passivity and timidity and never wanting to leave the house, and the Blue will probably hear something about how incredibly dull they can be. A real bore, to be honest.

You might also be subject to the silent treatment, which is so difficult in a relationship. The combination is extremely hard to handle.

Slowly but surely, it gets worse. Much worse. But there will always be instances when you will get the confirmation, the positive reinforcement that you need to feel good. Suddenly you will have a perfect romantic weekend, and you will be glowing again. Your partner is back to the kind, admiring, loving person you longed for. All hope is not lost! You still mean something to her! Until she withdraws again. And you find yourself back on that emotional roller-coaster ride.

You'll end up doing whatever she asks just to get back into her good graces.

ARE THERE ANY COUNTERMEASURES?

How can you avoid becoming a victim of a psychopath's love bombing? If you were ignorant of this unpleasant phenomenon, you would have no defense. But now that you are armed with a little knowledge, there are some things you can do.

As usual, it is a question of keeping a cool head. *If something sounds too good to be true, then it usually is*. Read that last sentence at least three times. Write it down and keep it in your wallet.

Let's Take a Closer Look at Trust

You know how it is with new acquaintances. It doesn't take long for us to make up our minds about someone. We are either for or against. We interact with extremely few people without making a judgment one way or another. Reflect on what it is that makes you trust a person. Because once you start to trust a person, you'll listen to them. So you need to be observant about what allows a particular person to gain your confidence. Once you've decided that a person is credible, reliable, and deserving of your trust, you already have a problem. Because everything that person says is going to be true.

This is how many dictatorships work. Dictators say everything their people want and need to hear, and thereby gain their trust. Then, bit by bit, they can start to carry out their long-term plans, consolidating power and removing their opposition.

Trust should not be granted for life. If a person gains your confidence, it does not mean you should uncritically believe everything that person says or does. You must be thoughtful enough to consider every single act separately and have the courage to question anything that seems strange—even if you're dealing with someone you actually trust. What I mean is that if someone is acting in a way that feels odd to you, reconsider that person's credibility, and do this regularly.

There Are Some Prerequisites for Trust

Confidence is built on three factors: predictability, reliability, and certainty.

Predictability is a consequence of your partner's behavior. It is the opposite of erratic or unpredictable behavior—for instance, positive reinforcement that comes and goes seemingly randomly, or expressions of love and tenderness that are suddenly exchanged for total silence and endless criticism without cause. When your darling's attitude and behavior switches on and off like that, the cause could very well be other than an attempt at manipulation, but be extremely observant of such behavior. A psychiatric diagnosis such as a bipolar disorder is one thing; psychopathy, quite another.

Reliability is what determines whether you can assume that your partner is honest and credible in the long term. Do you worry that you can't really rely on this person? What have you observed that confirms their long-term reliability? Did they behave one way during the first weeks, only to show their real identity later on, like a person lifting a mask? That is not a relationship worth having. If the person goes through heaven and hell with you and remains on your side, then you can feel fairly secure.

Certainty is about being convinced that your partner will meet your needs and that they can be relied on to act like a loving and supportive partner—for the long term and not just the first few months. Psychopaths don't have much patience, so they can't put on a show forever.

It is a mistake to base your judgment on your partner's earliest behavior when you decide whether they deserve your trust. Look at the three factors listed above: predictability, reliability, and certainty, and reflect on them in the *present*. Not last year or before you got married or how your partner behaved at home visiting your parents (your partner's behavior was probably exemplary, since a psychopath is careful to ensure that if something goes wrong, you will look like the bad guy). No, look at what happened this morning and yesterday and what is happening this very minute.

Is the behavior you have just observed worthy of your trust? Skillful manipulators are clever at gaining your trust, but they are actually hopeless at retaining it, since they will switch to negative behaviors as soon as they find an opportune moment. Don't fall for it.

Act Immediately!

Once you have seen through the psychopath's or the manipulator's trick, act forcefully and, above all, immediately. Psychologically, it's the same as being in a physically abusive relationship. Leave at the first blow.

I have never heard of someone only being hit once and then never again. That doesn't happen.

The same applies to psychological manipulation. If your partner displays that kind of behavior, then you can be 100 percent certain that it will be repeated. A psychopath or somebody with psychopathic traits will use the methods they know work. If they succeed in getting you to back down by manipulating you, why wouldn't they do it again? If a thief finds a hundred-dollar bill on the ground, picks it up, puts it in their pocket, and then has an evening out using somebody else's money, why would they step over the next hundred-dollar bill and leave it on the ground? You need to realize that the psychology is exactly the same. As they say: Fool me once, shame on you. Fool me twice, shame on me.

If someone manipulates you and you find out that there is only one correct response—leave.

How to Resist Being Manipulated

Act like a Red. Release your true emotions and act assertively and quickly. Save yourself from being reduced to a shadow of what you once were. Because that is what your partner is going to do with you. They will transform you into a pale copy of yourself. If you are feeling chronically insecure, unhappy, worried, or offended, you need to understand that you will be stuck in those feelings the longer you stay, which will make it harder and harder to see the game the psychopath is playing.

Remind yourself that a psychopath doesn't feel normal emotions—they just pretend. Remember that the person who is most committed to saving the relationship is the weaker party. The psychopath doesn't give a damn about you. Why give them a single minute of your life? You are worth so much more.

Technique 3: Negative Reinforcement

You would have thought this would be higher up on the list, right? But according to all those experts who have examined, investigated, and done research on manipulation, negative reinforcement is not necessarily the method of choice. And that says a lot about the human psyche.

The definition of negative manipulation is when the manipulator *stops* doing something you don't like when you *start* doing something they do like. And this has an extremely simple effect: In the future, you will do what the manipulator wants.

More Mice

Do you remember the laboratory mouse that ran from the black room to the white room? The researchers did, of course, test another variant: negative reinforcement. Don't just shoot the messenger. But what they did was to electrify the floor in the black room. When another mouse was put in there, it literally jumped around like it was crazy until it found the white door. Then it could escape from the torture chamber into the white room, where there wasn't any cheese—but where the floor didn't give them a mild electric shock. The reward was not a piece of cheese (positive reinforcement) but avoiding having electrical current under its feet (negative reinforcement).

But Humans Are Not Mice!

Let's say you're at work. If you write your weekly report in a way that your boss doesn't like, you will be publicly told off, and your work will be questioned. As soon as you adapt yourself to the new—though not necessarily better—method your boss prefers, the criticism will cease. Or if you question your boss during a meeting, you simply won't be invited to the next meeting. You might be shunned and have to suffer the silent treatment until you give in and go along with things.

But remember: This shouldn't be confused with ordinary, appropriate feedback that you actually deserve—for example, if you've missed a deadline on multiple occasions, don't keep to your budget, never deliver what you have promised, don't take care of the dissatisfied client, or cause trouble with coworkers for no reason. Or if you are one of the people who is trying to manipulate everyone around you.

I'm talking now about psychological manipulation, not consequences for poor work, and we need to keep the concepts clear.

What About on the Home Front?

In a relationship, things are more complicated, as usual: For example, perhaps you want to go out with the girls on a Friday evening but your boyfriend grumbles and argues and makes a scene until you call them and cancel, and he suddenly becomes happy again. Or if he tries to get you to go along with some sort of sexual activity that you don't enjoy, and when you decline, he won't touch you for weeks. (Many, often male, partners have a tendency to nag about various forms of sex that their partners aren't enthusiastic about, but this tactic is fairly obvious. That isn't necessarily manipulation but more what it sounds like—nagging. In such cases, you should just say no: "Don't bring that up again. I'm not interested.")

The negative-reinforcement tactic is as simple as it is effective. You will receive a negative response until you give in to whatever the manipulator asked for. Then everything will return to normal again. Remember what I said about predictability, reliability, and certainty. The same applies here.

And it really is simple. The manipulator knows that you're going to give in eventually to avoid the negative effects of their behavior. And once you've started giving in, there is a high likelihood that you'll continue to do so. And your behavior is now being decided by somebody other than you.

Are There Any Countermeasures?

You should react the same way as you would to an instance of arbitrary positive reinforcement. You need to learn to see through it. There are always partners and bosses around us who try to influence us; that's a given. Sometimes, it suffices to show that you realize what they're trying to do. If the perpetrator is a good person who isn't actually trying to deceive you, you'll hopefully have a good conversation where you can sort things out and move on.

You need to remember that manipulation often happens without the perpetrator intending it. If something works, then it works. You continue to press the same buttons. If you find something that gets you what you want, you keep doing it. A lot of people—that is, people who aren't psychopaths—don't realize the damage they are doing to their victim, but when you point it out, everything changes.

This is part of growing in any relationship, and nothing to worry about. And that's how you'll know if you're dealing with a psychopath or not. Because a psychopath won't apologize and change their actions. The psychopath will blame everything on you. It's your fault if your children don't talk with you, that you lost your job, that you're actually a pathetic, mean person who should be happy that somebody is prepared to have anything to do with you at all. You've abused the psychopath's kindness.

You can't change the other person, but you can take responsibility for yourself. Change your job. Get divorced. Abandon ship.

Technique 4: Unfathomable Smoke Screens

You're overreacting as usual! You're so unstable! Can't you see what a mess you're causing!

A skillful manipulator will say virtually anything to get you off-balance. The purpose is to shift the focus from the actual issue by claiming that you are the problem. This is normally accomplished by pressing various emotional buttons.

For example, if you suspect that your partner is unfaithful, you'll probably want to talk about it. You might manage to approach this conversation completely calmly. You just want to talk. But instead of talking about the real problem—infidelity—your partner simply denies everything and switches the focus onto you. Now they want to talk about your faults and shortcomings, such as your insecurity or jealousy. They might say that these traits are extremely unattractive. They're only saying this to sow even more doubt about your relationship, and you will immediately start wondering whether you're the one who is wrong after all.

Your suspicions about this infidelity might be well-founded, and who knows? You might be able to get into your partner's cell phone and find clear evidence of everything. That wouldn't be so surprising, since most psychopaths are incorrigibly promiscuous. What do you do? You confront him with what you have found.

He'll now switch to something completely different—the fact that you violated his privacy by looking at his cell phone. Now you have committed a serious wrong, and you will, ironically, be the one who is attacked for not trusting him. A manipulator, especially one who would score highly on the psychopath checklist, will do anything to switch the focus to something other than their wrongdoing.

When you are sucked into this confusing world, you need to be aware that the ordinary rules no longer apply.

A Particularly Unpleasant Example from Real Life

A woman I met a year or so ago told me the following story. Her husband had a pattern of always being short of money. He rarely had anything in his bank account, despite earning a good salary. He not only emptied their joint household account but even emptied the children's savings accounts. This man had always "forgotten" his wallet, and he took no responsibility for his money or for the family finances. In fact, the IRS was trying to track him down.

When the woman confronted him, he changed strategy completely.

He stood outside the children's room and started yelling at her. He shouted that everything he earned went to her and the children. Didn't she want their son to have his sport equipment? Or their other son to have his school laptop? The woman knew on a rational level that she was the one who had paid for everything, but the man's shouted accusations made her entirely lose focus on the real subject: his carelessness with money.

She suddenly found herself—in front of the children, on top of everything—forced to defend herself against the ridiculous claim that she didn't care for her family's well-being and happiness. But it didn't stop there. Her husband went on and bellowed that she didn't care about the children, that she didn't understand them, and that she was a cold and unfeeling mother. She only cared about herself!

What did any of this have to do with the fact that he was careless with money? Answer: absolutely nothing.

What had happened? Her husband didn't want to talk about the fact that he had taken large amounts from their joint account. Instead, he cast her as the villain—claiming she bought fancy bags and clothes for herself but wouldn't even allow him a new shirt. He would go into her closet and throw her clothes on the floor, shouting about how self-indulgent she was.

There was a grain of truth to his statements—she did buy lovely clothes using part of her salary. But what did that have to do with his spending money that was meant for the mortgage? These are two completely different topics. His accusation about her being a bad mother confused her and made her go on the defensive. And so he continued to burn through the family's money. To this day, nobody knows what he did with it all.

Are There Any Countermeasures?

You can be at the receiving end of smoke screens, regardless of which color you are. It's likely that Red and Blue people will find this technique slightly easier to deal with, but if things get very emotional—for instance, if your children become involved—you can't be sure of anything. Nobody is immune to psychopathy. You need to keep a cool, rational head when this happens. You need to observe every little deviation in the other party's behavior before you dare to confront them about what is happening.

You could say something like, "I noticed that you changed the subject. Can we finish what we were talking about?" Or, "Of course we can talk about your opinions, but first we are going to talk about the money that is missing." Or, "Why are you shouting at me? Stop shouting, and we can talk, but I will not put up with your shouting." Or the simplest of all: Leave the room, the house, the neighborhood. And broach the subject when other people are present. For example, at a restaurant or in the presence of somebody you trust. A mutual acquaintance, relative, or anybody whose presence ensures that this technique can't be used without the psychopath's making a complete fool of themselves.

The problem is that the psychopath will most likely have combined this technique with other methods of manipulation, so when they call you [fill in whatever you are most ashamed of about your personality], then you will instinctively back away.

Technique 5: Having Your Feelings
Turned Against You

Another way of creating confusion and distracting attention from the real issue is to turn your feelings against you. This tactic is also intended to divert your attention away from the real problem.

The tactic is about putting pressure on sensitive points in your personality, things that you perhaps are not especially proud of. The advantages for the manipulator are obvious: Emotions are difficult to handle. And difficult emotions are even harder. The psychopath knows that, so they force difficult emotions into the open to make you lose focus on the real issue.

If the manipulator is a man, he might make a sexist comment like, "Are you PMSing?" That's it. Classic domination technique. Or perhaps he'll simply say something he knows will provoke you and knock you off-balance.

Imagine a Red person, known for their aggressive temper. A hard nut to crack, one might think. But not really, not if the manipulator knows their victim well enough. What are Red people infamous for? Tactless and aggressive behavior. Normally, this doesn't bother them, but Red people who are self-aware know how their temper can hurt their loved ones.

This tactic works in two directions. On the one hand, the manipulator can simply encourage their Red victim to get angry by provoking them. Since the psychopath doesn't feel anything themselves, they can deal with the anger without a problem. And then they can instantly point the finger: "Look! That's exactly what I'm talking about! Now you're shouting again! You are always angry; you're crazy!"

And now the fight is all about the Red person's aggressiveness, instead of whatever it was the manipulator has done. And there are plenty of variations on this theme, but you get the idea.

But it even works in the other direction. If the manipulator knows that their Red victim thinks these shouting matches are exhausting and counterproductive, the manipulator will make comments like, "You aren't going to start an argument now, are you? Are you going to lose your temper again? Soon you'll be shouting at me like always . . ."

The Red decides not to fall into the trap and smothers their anger.

It's an enormous effort. It's like not being able to find a bathroom when you need one. The pressure is painful, and now the victim is no longer fully engaged in the discussion. If the Red has decided they're not going to lose their temper, it will take most of their focus and effort. It requires a lot of mental work to refrain from following your instincts.

If the manipulator's victim is Yellow, it would look a little different. If the manipulator were to make use of the first tactic and deliberately encourage a certain behavior, they could say things like, "Now, of course, you're going to start babbling about all sorts of stuff, and I won't even know what you're on about. Why do you always talk about yourself? If only you could learn to talk less and listen more. You never listen to me!"

This definitely targets the Yellow's weakness—they put themselves in the middle of things and don't listen to others. This, too, is a rather unflattering trait. The Yellow will react by talking faster and louder, and (to be honest) rather incoherently. Now the manipulator can calmly say, "What did I just say? You're babbling on about yourself! You don't care about anyone but yourself!"

The other variant is a bit like the tactic used in the Red case: "Can you be quiet just this once and let me talk? Hello!" This would work extremely well when combined with tears. The Yellow knows that they have tendencies to twist everything to be about them and now falls silent. They are braced to refrain from doing what their instincts tell them. It is a bit like slowly smothering somebody. What can the Yellow do with their frustration if they can't release it in the form of words? Everything will stay inside, and they will feel miserable. But the manipulator has efficiently silenced them.

The Green is sensitive and does completely different things. If a manipulator lives together with a Green victim, it won't be much of a fight. I wouldn't go so far as to say that Greens are the easiest victims to manipulate, but they are by nature flexible and try to accommodate other people. Unfortunately, this means it's often easy to take advantage of them for malicious purposes.

I've always found it hardest to give feedback to Greens, because they take offense at almost everything. You have to be careful not to offend them unnecessarily, or they will be crushed. So how can somebody be deliberately mean toward a Green person?

Oops! Now I made the mistake of thinking logically again. As if a psychopath would care about how other people feel! Naturally, the psychopath couldn't care less. Their Green husband or wife is just a tool to be used.

The manipulator would be able to switch the Green person's focus by saying, "You never say anything. You're so damned cowardly and always back down as soon as anyone disagrees with you. You refuse to have a productive discussion about anything. I'm so fed up with you!"

This is mostly true, and it would probably paralyze most Greens. The manipulator encourages exactly this behavior. The Green person withdraws and just sits there, possibly with tears welling up. Beneath the surface, they are boiling with frustration. There's so much they want to say, but how? They are too afraid of conflict.

But it's also possible to get a Green person to act against instinct. A really skillful manipulator can get a Green person so out of balance emotionally that they will erupt and start screaming. Everything would come out—every grievance, every slight, every disappointment. Their fury will go on for a while, and they will give the manipulator lots of valuable information that they can use later on.

The advantage for the manipulator is that the Green will feel ashamed afterward. Guilty and devastated, the Green will apologize for their conduct. The manipulator can now act the part of victim: *How could you be so cruel and hurtful? Poor me! You'll pay for this!*

What about the Blue? How can a manipulator turn the Blue's conduct against them? Simple. By pressing the most sensitive buttons that the Blue has. This is more difficult at a workplace, as I've shown earlier. One effective method is to continually put them in situations where they don't feel comfortable. Like making them work on projects with only Yellow people. Or forcing them into a presentation they are completely unprepared for. This would be preceded by the boss saying, "Now I don't want to see one of your boring, fact-filled presentations. I want to see a light touch and a bit of humor. Do you understand? Get up there now."

Of course, Blue persons have a sense of humor, but to expect them to be brilliant entertainers is asking too much. They'd probably get up on stage, but who knows how it would end? And when they are deliberately trying to not be themselves, they won't be able to function. The presentation will be drier than ever, because they aren't spontaneous—like a Yellow person. It's just not who they are. Afterward, the boss can criticize them endlessly for their poor performance.

However, a Blue person can handle this. Their relationship with their colleagues or bosses isn't as important to them as it is for many others. In a close relationship, they are just as vulnerable as anybody else.

Say that a Blue's girlfriend wants him to do something he doesn't feel like doing. Let's say that she wants to travel to Paris for a romantic weekend. There is going to be a lot of expensive shopping—after all, this is Paris we're talking about. And he knows from experience that she is going to "forget" her credit card at home. It's going to cost a whole month's salary, since she's chosen the most expensive hotel, and she expects him to pay for the whole thing.

At the first suggestion of the trip, he gets a bit of a stomachache. His girlfriend knows exactly how he is going to answer, so she demands in an emotional way that he doesn't get out his calculator and start going through the costs. She insists that he listen to her and show some interest for once. Since he loves his girlfriend, he listens (he can do the math in his head). So he adds up the expenses while she rattles off all her demands. When he tells her that it costs too much and just isn't feasible, she does what she's planned the whole time: Accuse him of having no feelings. *How can he be so cold toward her? If he loves her, he would give her this for once.* (Fact: They usually go on a trip like this every year, so this is not a one-time thing.)

If he still doesn't give in, she'll use the weapon that not even Blue people can defend against: She'll start crying. Sentimental nonsense. A pain to deal with. He suffers through the outburst and starts wondering whether he can take on even more overtime to get enough money for a trip he doesn't even want to take.

Technique 6: The Triangle Drama

The triangle drama is an extremely underhanded yet also effective tactic designed to confuse you and make you feel uncertain. It can be used successfully at your workplace but is most effective in a private relationship. The manipulator creates a situation involving you and them, along with a third party who has nothing to do with you.

In a relationship, this is a dreadful weapon, especially in combination with other techniques. Imagine that your partner has complimented you for months (positive reinforcement), but has suddenly gone silent. You've tried to earn back their affection and praise without success. Instead, your partner has given you a lot of unexpected, harsh criticism (negative reinforcement). You're confused and hurt. Things that your partner loved about you months ago are now evidently serious flaws. And the last weekend has been marked by silence—complete silence.

With a sinking feeling in your stomach, you try to talk with your partner: What's the matter?

Instead of answering your worried questions, the manipulator now starts to talk about a completely different person, a third party you didn't even know existed. It could be an old flame or a female colleague he has started to work with—anyone at all. And he goes on all week about this woman, merrily informing you about how nice she is, how easy it is to talk with her, and how positive she is about everything. He will likely describe this woman as a person with qualities that are diametrically opposed to yours. If you're Yellow, the woman he works with will be Blue. If you are Green, the woman he describes is Red. What would that feel like? To not react to his baiting, you'd have to be made of stone.

If, however, you're like most people, your insecurity is going to go through the roof, and your desire to please your manipulative partner will be even higher. Whatever they ask for, you'll tie yourself in knots trying to deliver exactly that. And why not? Relationships take work, right? To get something to really succeed, you have to try a bit harder; everyone says that. But that can't be your task alone. It has to come from both parties.

If you were to confront your manipulative partner with all this—for example, after having read this book and realizing that you've been subjected to a constructed triangle drama—they will simply deny everything. *You're imagining things. You're jealous, and you need to work on your low self-esteem.*

The Double Bluff

What's particularly horrible about this scenario is that it's not uncommon for the manipulator to actually be spending their spare time with this third person while simultaneously dangling them in your face. Psychopaths do love excitement, and they don't have any problem taking enormous risks. So they'll happily flirt and build a relationship with the third person right in front of your nose while pushing you right over a cliff of jealousy. If you confront them with all of this, you'll get to hear that you are just behaving jealously and that, once again, your fragile self-esteem is the problem. This may even be what they use as a reason to end your relationship. And you will continue to live your life believing that it was your fault.

(I might add here that there are, of course, lots of people who are habitually jealous of their partners without having grounds for it. But that is something entirely different. Sometimes, you've just ended up living with a jealous bastard. Leave him. Or her.)

In a sound relationship, none of this happens. In a functional relationship, both parties (not just one) make an effort to allow their partner to feel secure and confident, and the triangle drama doesn't exist. Should the worry crop up and you're living with a "normal" person and not with a psychopath, you'll be able to sort things out fairly simply. Your husband realizes that you don't want to hear about Lisa's merits all the time. He'll remind himself to also compliment you for being the person you are. If he's normal.

In personal relationships we're all susceptible to this type of manipulation. All of us have something to lose, and virtually anyone can feel jealousy when they're in love. If you're feeling jealous, it isn't related to your color so much as it is to fear of losing the person you love, or think you love. But if you could look inside the manipulator's head, love would most likely be swapped for something else.

Triangle Drama at Your Workplace?

The triangle drama can be just as effective at work. Your boss, who always used to think well of you, suddenly has a new favorite. Johnny, the new guy, now gets lots of the same sort of praise that you used to get. *Okay,* you think, *but he's very sharp, after all.* Nothing strange in that. He seems to be clever and sympathetic, so there isn't really anything to say about it.

But if your boss is a psychopath (or has psychopathic traits), he will take some of your usual assignments and give them to Johnny. It might look as if the boss wants to lighten your load—you've worked so hard, after all—but it's only the fun and important work tasks that end up with Johnny. You don't understand and ask Johnny, "Why are you doing my job?" He, however, didn't even know these tasks were yours; he is new, after all. You can't blame him.

You go to the boss and ask what's happening. The boss says that you're being ungrateful if you don't want to help develop a new co-worker. *How can you be so selfish? Besides, Johnny is good at his job, don't you think?* Perhaps the boss gives you a meaningful look and says that "it's a rather urgent project, too." You have to admit to yourself that you're a bit of a time optimist and have difficulties meeting a deadline, as well as a tendency to revise things more than necessary.

Besides, Johnny does extremely high-quality work, and when your boss points this out while giving you a thoughtful look, you start doubting. Perhaps you aren't as good as you thought you were.

At meetings, the boss now brags about Johnny, just like he used to brag about you. This will bother you, because you've now lost something. And in combination with other manipulation techniques, such as positive reinforcement and negative reinforcement, your downhill journey is starting. It doesn't matter why your boss does this. He'll probably have his reasons, and what these are doesn't really matter. Perhaps you questioned him one time too many, or he might simply be bored.

If your boss is a real psychopath, he won't need any special reason. He'll do it because it amuses him. He might give your job to a person he can control more easily. Perhaps he simply wants to see how far he can push you; psychopaths see the rest of us as material to use and discard as the mood strikes them.

Who Will Get Caught by this Technique?

How do the different colors react here? The danger can be greatest for Red and Yellow people. Their egos are by nature fairly strong, and when they are called into question on the professional level, that's rarely good news. The Red, whose self-image is that of a natural winner, is extremely provoked and will probably show it. If they have a lively temperament, then things can get quite hot.

The problem here is evident: It plays straight into the hands of the psychopathic boss. Losing your temper at work is very unprofessional (even though the boss will certainly use anger as a weapon), and the boss will naturally ask the Red to pull it together. Just look at how calmly and politely Johnny is behaving. Why can't you be as professional as he is?

The Yellow, however, who is especially positive about their own skills, will immediately feel bad if they lose their status among the staff. They're used to being the person that everyone turns to. But since the boss is always praising Johnny—perhaps at the same time spreading far-from-positive rumors about the Yellow, which will further strengthen the message that the Yellow employee won't be with the company long, the Yellow will lose even more ground, and their effectiveness will continue to plummet.

Suddenly, all their thoughts will turn to the situation and why they have suddenly found themselves in it. They'll spend all day parsing how this whole mess was created. The Yellow can now become extremely passive and lose their sense of direction. This, too, will be exploited by the boss. Now the field is open to criticize the Yellow for late deliveries, and when the boss does this in public, the Yellow will be crushed. Public criticism is the same as humiliation. For a Yellow individual, the loss of status is a hard blow. Now they are disgraced and their self-image is cracking.

A Green coworker will, however, react differently. They didn't even want to be the center of attention to start with, so that particular bit is of no relevance. It would actually be nice to avoid having so much focus on them for a while. On the other hand, the Green wants more quiet reinforcement. So when those pleasant, slightly informal meetings with the boss stop altogether, they can start worrying. If their self-confidence has already been a little diminished, it will now get knocked down further.

The difference is that the Green rarely asks for anything. Having never demanded something of their boss, they are hardly going to confront the boss now and ask for positive feedback. And raising the problem itself is unthinkable. The Green's fear of conflict limits their response to this type of issue.

They will go to their usual allies in the office, the people they normally confide in. But since these people are presumably also Green, problems can arise: They won't want the boss to be dissatisfied with them, so they won't stick up for their poor colleague or will even withdraw from that person altogether. Our Green friend might be under the impression that they have the support of their coworkers, when they don't have any at all. Their mates might well have changed sides—perhaps gone over to Johnny's—without the Green having noticed. If the malevolent boss continues with the same tactic or perhaps combines it with alternating negative feedback, the Green is going to be miserable. They don't have the same drive as the Reds and the Yellows to help them. This can eventually lead to burnout and extreme mental stress.

But what about the Blue coworker? I know you've begun to understand the pattern. The Blue person is less likely to react to some things. Losing their status within the group is not a problem for them. Not being asked for their opinion on important issues can also be okay. After all, they know what they know. It also doesn't matter to them very much if they become distant from others in the group. There was too much small talk in the building anyway. So the Blue can live with the fact that their psychopathic boss has succeeded in getting the group to turn against them and to prefer Johnny. They might never have been part of the group in the first place.

The problem will be if the quality of their work is called into question. When the boss uses Johnny as a third party and tries to make the Blue's work look subpar, he will target the quality of the Blue's work. The worst thing you can do to a Blue person is accuse them of carelessness and sloppiness. These are behaviors the Blue would never exhibit, and the accusation will hit them hard. They'll probably react by becoming even more silent. They were taciturn before; now they're silent as a stone.

Technique 7: Gaslighting

This technique is very interesting. The term has its origins in a film from the 1930s with Ingrid Bergman, where she plays a woman whose husband tries to drive her mad by changing things around her all the time while denying that anything is different. In the film, he turns the flame in the gaslight up and down continuously, until she can no longer rely on her own senses. The term *gaslighting* thus refers to the tactic of completely distorting a victim's sense of reality and making them question their own sanity.

Gaslighting, in the hands of a manipulator, is a slow and extremely advanced tactic.

A Simple Example

One way of gaslighting is the way it was done in the old film: moving physical objects. For example, a framed picture that is hanging a bit crooked hardly sounds like a major problem. But if you adjust it so that it's level and then the next day find that it's crooked again, how many times can this happen before you go to your partner and raise the issue? *You know that painting I got from my grandmother, it's somehow crooked every day!* Your partner doesn't understand what you're talking about. He hasn't seen anything wrong with the painting, ever. You both go and have a look. It's hanging level. *Okay*, you might think, this time. But the same evening the painting is crooked again. If your partner were to move the painting from hanging level to crooked every time you raised the issue, how long would it be before you started wondering if you had imagined the whole thing? After all, isn't it weird that you're the only one alone who sees the crooked painting?

The above example is, of course, simplified, and I don't think you need to worry that your partner will drive you to madness with a portrait of Grandpa Jack. The trick with the crooked painting might not send many of us to a mental hospital. But it's a good description of how gaslighting works.

Let's look at how it might function in a more complex situation.

A Subtle Example

Say that you live with a psychopath. He tells you that for Christmas he is going to give you the fanciest present you've ever received. You're excited and immediately think it must be that wonderful handbag from Louis Vuitton you've dreamed of for years. The handbag costs several thousand dollars, and you've never owned anything that nice. The psychopath goes with you to the shop, and you order the handbag together—it will even have your monogram on it. The shop's staff smile, and everybody is pleased; you're ecstatic and thrilled. Such a beautiful handbag! You've found your dream partner; he's so generous!

But when it's time to pay for the bag, it turns out that the psychopath doesn't have any money. In confusion, you look at the handbag, at your psychopathic partner, at the sales assistant . . . and finally pull out your own credit card. Otherwise, it would be just absolutely humiliating. In the car on your way home, you cautiously raise the question: It was a present, wasn't it? Your partner gives you a questioning look. *What are you talking about? How could I afford such an expensive present?*

You are 100 percent certain that he promised you the bag as a gift. But now he says that he would never do such a thing. You start wondering whether you somehow misunderstood him. But he seems so convinced he's right. And he doesn't usually give you expensive presents. Who has misunderstood whom here?

Another example: Your wife gets all dressed up one evening to go out with her girlfriends. You ask her why she didn't mention her plans before, and she answers: "Of course I did. We talked about this last week." You might argue back, because you definitely wouldn't forget something like that. On the other hand, you have forgotten things before, and nobody is perfect.

Regardless, she tells you she'll be with Anna and heads out.

Anna is married to your friend, so when it gets very late and your wife hasn't come home and isn't answering your texts, you phone your friend to ask if Anna is back. He replies that Anna has been at home all evening.

What the . . . ! What on earth is happening? You immediately suspect there is something fishy going on. Is your wife having an affair with another man?

When she comes home in the middle of the night, you're upset and accuse her of having lied to you. She hasn't been out with Anna at all! Since your wife is a psychopath, she will look you in the eye and insist she didn't say Anna; she said Anneli. You are completely sure she never said Anneli, and anyway who the hell is Anneli?

Now your wife adopts a different tactic. She hammers away where you're weakest. If you're Red, she'll say that you're an insensitive jerk who never listens; if you are Yellow, she will claim that you only think of yourself and question why you haven't managed to remember the names of her friends; if you are Green, she will simply shout at you, since you're afraid of conflict; if you're Blue, she might start to question your mental ability and question whether you are senile.

The Psychology Behind It

Gaslighting is about creating confusion: saying A on Monday and B on Tuesday and then, on Wednesday, claiming neither A nor B was ever said. In the beginning, you might be able to keep up, but after a while you'll start losing your grasp of what has (or hasn't) been said. It will all become confused. Unfortunately, in combination with other techniques, this is going to work. And a skillful psychopath will build up over time. They start on a small scale—just a few inconsistencies here and there—and then gradually increase the confusion. Bit by bit, this method will creep up on you, and finally you won't know whether you're coming or going.

Let's involve a few more people. The psychopath that is your partner has said one thing to you, but something quite different to your mother. Or to your children. When you later tell them about something you know he said, the others—who are being completely manipulated by the psychopath—will think you've gotten everything completely wrong.

At a workplace, this is really destructive. Imagine a psychopathic boss who wants to get rid of someone who has worked there a very long time. Perhaps they're just tired of the employee in question, or perhaps that person has questioned their authority. Or maybe the boss would tick off every item in the psychopathy checklist and just likes destroying people's lives.

How will the boss get rid of this employee? By making them completely and utterly confused. The coworker will not be invited to a key meeting. Important information will be withheld from them. After the meeting, when the coworker realizes they were excluded, they will ask their boss about it. The boss says that somebody else was responsible for the invitations. There must have been a mistake. The coworker then goes to the person who organized the meeting and learns that the boss had specifically said that the coworker should not be invited. Back to the boss, who of course denies everything. If you keep pushing, you might find yourself in even bigger trouble.

You can imagine what a nightmare it would be. And a boss who consistently operates in this manner will create enormous confusion. In the end, nobody will trust anybody else.

A skillful psychopath will make use of several techniques at the same time. And soon the whole team will think that you're really losing it. You can't be relied on. You're always making accusations, especially against the boss, who's been nothing but kind and sympathetic. All the pawns rush to his rescue. Regardless of color, you risk finding yourself on sick leave at the end of your career.

Gaslighting is a monstrous tactic that does permanent damage to people. It is a horrible and manipulative domination technique, and it works because psychopaths lie all the time.

If somebody in your vicinity should attempt this and you are able to detect the pattern: Get out of there! I can't understate the importance of this. You're dealing with a disturbed person; you don't want to have anything to do with them.

Technique 8: The Silent Treatment

If you are mainly Green or Blue, the above head won't seem especially frightening. With the TV and radio full of people who like nothing better than hearing their own voices, nowadays silence is a gift. How often have you wished someone would just, *please,* be quiet.

On the other hand, being on the receiving end of what psychologists call passive-aggressive behavior is something entirely different. It includes having to suffer the silent treatment, never having your questions answered, and being ignored so completely that it can drive you mad.

As a result of something you have done or not done, your manipulator will become silent, withdraw, and not answer when spoken to as a way of punishing you. Everyone who has gone through this will know exactly what I'm talking about.

In one of my earlier relationships, my partner used this technique very frequently. It wasn't psychopathy in that particular instance, but it was undoubtedly a manipulative behavior.

Imagine that you and your partner disagree on a certain issue. It doesn't matter who's right or wrong, but your partner gives you the silent treatment until you simply give in. No greetings, no "good morning," no "good night," no "goodbye" when your partner leaves home. And physical contact? Forget it. The manipulator's goal is to effectively kill all communication between you. They won't answer the phone if you call them; they won't reply to your text messages. If you ask what's wrong, you'll only get a murderous look in return. The point of this is to make you feel invisible and powerless. And I can promise you, it does work. This unpleasant method gives rise to everything from feelings of guilt to utter shame.

How mean have I really been?

This behavior is extremely difficult for the person at the receiving end. The manipulator refuses to confirm your existence, and after a few days of silence you're ready to do anything at all to get some sign of life back. Often that means you show up with flowers and presents and grovel like a worm on the ground.

Some psychologists call this emotional torture. If it sounds exaggerated, I would remind you of something called Chinese water torture. It doesn't sound so bad, but it can drive a person completely mad. The victim was placed lying on their back with their face under a barrel filled with water. The barrel had a tap that leaked one drop of water a minute. Each individual drop was hardly felt, and one hour under the barrel might not have been so bad. But what about a whole week? Prisoners who were tortured in this way sometimes went mad. A tiny drop, but an enormous effect on the victim. That's exactly how silence works.

There's no doubt that I was hurt by having been the victim of the silent treatment a number of times. Together with other methods, this technique is very effective.

As usual, it will cease when you give in and do what the manipulator wants. The solution is to confront the manipulator with what he or she is doing and hope that they stop doing it.

Some More Manipulation Techniques

What I've described above are some of the more complicated techniques a manipulator makes use of. There are, of course, many more variations. Here's a list of a selection of them, together with a brief description of what they involve:

- Indiscretion. Early in your relationship, the psychopath reveals personal details (whether true or false) about themselves and encourages you to share similarly private things about yourself, things they will later use against you—for example, "My father always shouted at me, and I hate it when somebody raises their voice."
- Putting the blame on the victim. Regardless of what isn't working in your relationship, the psychopath will find ways of blaming everything on you.
- Indirect insults. Mean criticism that is hidden behind fake concern—for example, "Maybe you should go back to bed, sweetheart. You look a little haggard this morning."
- Insinuating comments or compliments. A way of expressing themselves so ambiguously that you don't know whether they intended a comment as a compliment or an insult—for example, "You know what, you could earn lots of money as a prostitute!"
- Creating guilty feelings. Accusing the victim of being mean or unfair toward the manipulator—for example, "How can you accuse me of that? When I've always done everything for you!"

- Empty words. Psychopaths don't place any value in what they say. They can express themselves any way they want depending on the situation—for example, "I love you." This will keep you calm for the time being, but it doesn't mean anything, because the psychopath doesn't love.

- Making light of their particular action. The psychopath forcefully convinces you that what they did wasn't a big deal: "So what, everyone does that, right?" "But nothing happened!"

- Telling lies. How to distinguish the lies from everything else is tricky, but if you notice some of the methods listed above, then you can be sure that the psychopath also lies to you. About everything. All the time. Don't trust a single thing they say.

- Making light of everything you think, feel, and experience—for example, "You shouldn't worry about that" or "You must be joking. That wasn't a big deal at all!"

- Charm. Not to be forgotten! The psychopath begins by charming you. They say things you've never heard before. And you'll be enchanted because it feels so good.

- Forgetfulness (deliberate, that is). The psychopath will simply forget to fetch your clothes from the dry cleaner. Or to buy your favorite jam. Or to phone home from the hotel.

- Anger. Starting to shout and yell to force you to back down if you stand up against the psychopath's madness.

- Acting the part of the victim. Even though psychopaths can't feel sorry for themselves, they can play the role of a victim just as well as anybody else—for example, "I'm so stupid, I should have known better than to borrow your father's car. Look, now I've got it scratched in the parking lot. You'll hate me for this!"

- Rationalization. A common defense mechanism, but here it's used deliberately. It means fabricating a logical explanation for illogical behavior—for example, "All men look at pornography!" or "Sorry I hit you, but I got so angry when you provoked me."

- Flattery. Does that need any explanation? We all know what it feels like when somebody praises our appearance, our body, our intelligence, or our taste. Psychopaths know it, too. Don't fall for it!

There are, of course, even more ways to manipulate somebody, but the book would be too long if I listed them all. If you want to know more, check out the bibliography at the end.

In the next chapter, I explain what you can do to counter all these unpleasant methods. Let us join the resistance movement!

16

Everyday Manipulation and How to Handle It

She said if you're beginning to feel worried that you may be a psychopath, if you recognize some of those traits in yourself, if you're feeling a creeping anxiety about it, that means you are not one.

—Jon Ronson, *The Psychopath Test: A Journey Through the Madness Industry*

Not all the people who are manipulative and behave badly are psychopaths. Some have psychopathic traits, while others are just generally lacking in charm and are unaware of their own conduct. They might suffer from narcissism or an exaggerated belief in their own abilities, or perhaps they tend to lie more than is acceptable. Many people indulge in conscious or unconscious manipulation of their partner, for example. All these small peculiarities are parts of the psychopathic personality. However, each on its own is just an unpleasant trait and not a reason to leave town. We'll take a look at these qualities now.

What can you do if you happen to run across one of these people? What can you do if you meet somebody who isn't actually a psychopath but who behaves like a real bastard nonetheless?

You have two choices:

1. Offer resistance
2. Leave

If you think that there is still hope, I'd like to give you support. So let's bring the resistance movement to life. For example, if you're in a relationship that is going off the rails, where the balance of power is leaning dangerously toward your partner, you *can* resist and make them own up to their actions.

Fight back . . . or leave? That's the question.

You might think it's easy to answer that. Or you might think this is the wrong question to ask—we should expect some struggle in a relationship. And, indeed, if your partner isn't a psychopath, then the situation will benefit from a constructive approach. But if you're going to succeed, you'll need some ammunition. So here it is.

The advantage to resisting (that is, clearly and decisively showing that you will no longer respond to the manipulator's dirty tricks) is that the manipulator must now make a choice of their own: They can adapt to the changes you demand by starting to conduct themselves more respectfully and contributing to a healthier balance between you. Or the manipulator may also tire of your resistance and simply move along to another victim, a victim who is most likely already somewhere in the background and will now become the focus of their attention. If they choose the latter, then you'll know that your partner is a psychopath. A true psychopath is not going to change their behavior. They may act "cured" for a few weeks, but you'll soon be back to where you were before.

Regardless of what choice the manipulator makes, your resistance will initially be met with dodging and shifting as the manipulator tries to avoid responsibility. This could result in a minor war between you, and I would be lying if I didn't say that it could all end up a dreadful mess. Your relationship could fall apart because your roles are too ingrained in your shared history.

If, however, you succeed in your resistance, the balance of power in your relationship will change. Initially, this can be rather hard to deal with, because it means you will suddenly have far more responsibility. But if you believe in the relationship, it will be worth the effort.

1. Break the Pattern

The usual response when you find yourself the target of manipulation is to react directly. If somebody shouts at you, you might burst into tears or shout back—*directly*. If somebody accuses you of something you haven't done, you defend yourself—*directly*. If you catch somebody in a lie, you will want to confront them—*directly*. If you see your partner flirt with another person at a party, you will want to walk across the room and slap them—*directly*.

A more effective method is to postpone your immediate response and allow time to pass between the event and your reaction to what happened.

The problem with responding too fast is that you are reacting exactly as the manipulator wants you to. Remember that we're probably talking about a person who knows you better than you know yourself. You need time to think. Reflect on what happened and plan your response. Don't react with a gut feeling or instinctively. Stop and think.

Since you're accustomed to giving a certain response to certain behaviors—to always answer yes to certain questions—you need a few helpful techniques.

For example, a telephone is a perfect way to slow down a conversation that is happening too fast. It might be that your darling wants to buy something expensive with your money and tries the "I promise to pay you back as soon as my salary arrives" line with you or that your boss has used some dirty trick to back you into a corner so that you'll have no choice but to shoulder a project that will require days of unpaid overtime.

Your immediate response ought to be:

- "You'll have to wait a minute. Sorry."
- "Someone just walked into my office; I've got to hang up. Ring me in five minutes."
- "My battery is running out. I've got to find my charger—I'll phone you later."

Sometimes even this little technique is difficult. Note that you're not asking for anybody's permission. You've just excused yourself and hung up without being unpleasant. You informed them that you're going to need a couple of minutes for something else. This is the breathing space you need to break the pattern. Meanwhile, you'll have time to think through what was said and how you *ought* to react to it.

If it's a text message, it shouldn't bother you in the slightest. Just ignore it; don't reply. Or wait an hour or two. I have a couple of friends who usually answer text messages at lightning speed. You might think this shows that they're exceptionally efficient, but it also suggests an inability to think through their answers. Sometimes it can lead to disastrous consequences.

Talking face-to-face is more of a challenge—this requires a certain finesse. But why not go grab some more coffee, duck into the bathroom, or greet a person whom you've never seen before. Pick up your cell phone and discover an urgent email that you must answer immediately. The effect is the same: You get a bit of a breathing space to think.

Just do that. *Think.*

Even if this technique sounds ridiculously simple for some of you, for others it might be very scary. You know that there can be consequences if you don't play along. It will feel uncomfortable. But you know this is exactly what you need to do. Because there is something wrong.

If you can't get your thoughts together even after a minute has passed, you can always continue to refuse to give any response:

- "I need time to think through what you just said, so I'll have to get back to you when I've finished thinking through things."
- "That question requires a lot of consideration, so I need time to think it over. I'll get back to you as soon as I can. Thanks for understanding."
- "I can't give you an answer just now. I'll definitely give your proposal some thought, and I'll get back to you as soon as I possibly can."
- "This sounds like an important matter, and I'm going to need a bit of time to give it the attention it deserves. Then, of course, I'll get back to you."

If you're Red, you'll likely have already moved on to the next chapter, but could I ask you to consider my suggestion? You're already painfully aware of how your feeling of urgency has worked against you, and your lack of interest in details has probably cost you a pretty penny. You know that you respond too quickly—sometimes even before you've understood the question you've been asked.

If you're Yellow, you might be wondering how you can keep your mouth shut. Lots and lots of unprocessed thoughts fall out of your mouth without your noticing. But you also know, if you allow yourself a few moments of reflection, that your quick tongue has gotten you in trouble on occasion. Hasn't it? Stop and think!

If you're Green, do what you're best at. Don't answer at all. Ignore your inherent fear of conflict and make use of the Green's foremost weapon: passive-aggressive behavior. I want you to simply shake your head and say that you'll sleep on it. Don't say yes if you mean no. Repeat that ten times.

Finally, if you are Blue, perhaps you've already seen the logic behind my suggestion. You don't have any problem staring at the manipulator and thinking through things. You're not disturbed by silent pauses, and you have a neat and concrete solution—empirically tested—to fall back on if somebody tries to force you to give a quick answer.

Sure. If "your" manipulator is skilled, they'll question what you're doing. Your partner who wants to "borrow a thousand dollars from you until next pay day" will yell that they always pay you back, even if this isn't close to the truth. Your mother will burst into tears and wonder how you could be so heartless; she's always given you the very best. Your boss will threaten to give that fantastic project to somebody else, perhaps even tempt you by vaguely dangling the prospect of promotion in front of you.

Don't fall for it.

We are talking about manipulators. They're not to be trusted. If you're dealing with a psychopath, it's especially dangerous to give in straightaway. Then you've given them yet another weapon for their arsenal.

Don't expect to remain calm and balanced through it all. You might well be forced to hide in the bathroom for real. And the manipulator won't give up immediately; they'll try something else that has always worked on you. They want to get their own way. They are used to getting their own way. They *intend* to get their own way.

The breathing space that you are going to create won't last long. I don't want to lie to you; there's going to be a bit of saber-rattling for a while. But remember this: Your newly aroused resistance is due to the fact that you are not comfortable in the relationship you're in. It's dysfunctional, and you want things to change. Stand firm and stay strong.

Remember this too: If you do the same that you've always done, you'll get what you've always gotten.

A tip: Your *behavior* needs to be changed and first your feelings about the situation need to change. That's how we function. So don't give up.

2. Become a Broken Record

Young people today hardly know what a record is, but the rest of us remember the expression "he sounds like a broken record."

The phrase was used to describe someone who repeated the same line again and again. In this case, that's the goal. I want you to be like a broken record: Repeat your message time after time after time.

Why? Because your manipulator is a master at subjecting you to pressure you can't resist. But you must resist. You don't have to explain yourself. You can simply repeat that you'll get back to them on the issue. No apologies or long-winded explanations are necessary. Repeat the same thing five hundred times if need be.

> *I'll get back to you on this when I have finished thinking things over.*

Full stop.

It's extremely important that you do *not* get entangled in a dialogue around *why* you're not giving an answer to the original question, nor should you start discussing *when* you will be giving them an answer. You would lose control again; the conversation would only tip over to your disadvantage; and—oops—just like always, you'll have gone along with something you wanted to avoid.

> *I'll get back to you on this when I have finished thinking things over.*

That's it.

Be consistent. Don't change the message. Stand firm. Don't change your mind. People who do exactly what they say they're going to do are respected by others. If you show that you suddenly won't give in to pressure in the form of tears, shouting, threats, promises, or whatever normally works on you, you'll suddenly find yourself in control. Make sure you retain that control.

Don't change your mind. Be consistent. The power of consistency is enormous.

This is what a broken record sounds like:

The Manipulator (M): *You're so good at getting things sorted out that I've decided you should plan the ENTIRE party!*

You: *I've got to take another call. Sorry.* (Breathe deeply and think about whether you want to take on this suicide mission or not.) . . . *Thanks for hanging on. I need a bit of time to think about your suggestion. I'll get back to you as soon as I can.*

M: (already irritated, presumably): *Think about what? Do you mean that you aren't going to take responsibility for the party?*

You: *I understand that you're surprised* (recognizing what might be the manipulator's genuine feeling), *but I need to think this over, so I'll get back to you.*

M: *Well, I can't wait very long. There isn't much time to play with here. Which is precisely why I need you for the planning. I really need to know your answer now.*

You: *I understand that you're worried, but I need time to think this over. I'll get back to you as soon as I can.*

M: (now presumably a bit angry at the sudden opposition): *You're being completely unreasonable. I need your help here,*

*and you're landing me in a mess. What's your problem? What
do you need to think over? There's nothing to think over!*

You: (deep breath): *I understand your frustration, but I'll get
back to you later. Bye.*

And I suggest that you hang up at this point.

You could, of course, tell this person to go to hell from the very
start. The problem is that you are risking your relationship, and the
person may not be aware of their manipulative methods.

The power of consistency. Write that down.

3. Deprogramming Fear, Worry, and Guilt

Fear is often about something real, such as the fear of being rejected,
the fear of making a mistake, the fear of not being accepted, the fear
of criticism, the fear of conflict, the fear of somebody else's anger, the
fear of being isolated from the group—to list a few of the fears that
most of us can recognize in ourselves.

Worry is a variety of fear, but it is often abstract. In most cases,
one worries about something that never happens. The worry that my
child will be born with only nine fingers, the worry of crashing the
car, the worry of losing your job, and so on.

But—and this is a fact—most of what we worry about never happens. Look back at your life so far and reflect on some of the things
you've worried about over the years. You will realize that only a small
fraction of your worry was justified. (That's why I usually say that
optimists are realists, since they assume that everything will work
out perfectly all right, which it does in most cases. The pessimists, the
people who call themselves realists, have no sense of reality.) Worry
is almost always unjustified.

Guilt is a particular problem in our part of the world (as opposed to other parts of the world, where shame is a worse problem). Guilt is something that only humans suffer from. Animals don't. Guilt is, for example, the feeling of being responsible because someone is unhappy, the idea that it's your fault if I'm sad or feel I've been badly treated.

Skillful manipulators, as I have said before, want to get you off-balance, and they know how to subject you to one or even all of these negative feelings. They can shout, threaten, sniffle, cry, or play both the victim and the martyr to make you feel worry, fear, or guilt. And until now it's worked.

What the Reds Fear

If you're Red, just think about everything that you don't have control over to find out what you fear. I know that you aren't going to show it, but don't try to claim that you don't feel it sometimes; you're not totally devoid of feeling. Red people are generally afraid of losing control over the important things in their lives.

What the Yellows Fear

If you're Yellow, you are always going to be afraid of being rejected. If all your friends turned their backs on you, who would you be then? Isolation is the worst thing that can happen to a Yellow person. Look at the example (imaginary, but realistic nevertheless) of Lars and Anna earlier in the book. She managed to isolate him, which is what finally undid him.

What the Greens Fear

If you're Green, you will be afraid of conflict. Even a slightly raised voice will make you weak at the knees, and that's not a good feeling. Besides, you're afraid of anything changing too quickly. You'll back down if somebody threatens to shake your world too much.

What the Blues Fear

The Blue person is afraid of one thing more than anything else: being made a fool. This can be about work, about something in a relationship, or just the fear of looking totally clueless. So they'll go to considerable lengths to ensure that this doesn't happen. Making a fool of themselves and being caught with their pants down would be a humiliation they would never forget.

What's the Worst that Can Happen?

Once you've made up your mind to sever the manipulator's power over you, a lot of these feelings will surface: You're going to be worried about what will happen; you are going to be afraid of concrete repercussions. Worst of all: You're going to feel some guilt because, for once, you're thinking about yourself.

Don't misunderstand me: I am not imagining that you're a perfect person. You have your faults and shortcomings just like I have mine, but being manipulated and tricked is not something that you deserve. So, during the process of liberating yourself from the grasp of the manipulator, you need to think about your own well-being for a period. As time goes by, you'll work on your weaknesses and develop the person you are. But that comes later.

One thing you do need to deal with directly is your ability to resist these unpleasant feelings. Carrying a burden of fear, worry, and guilt is very hard to bear. Believe me, I've tried all three. During a period in my life, I was an expert on worry. But that was before I realized that most of what I was worried about never occurred.

In Susan Jeffers's excellent bestseller *Feel the Fear—and Do It Anyway*, she describes how you can handle these feelings, and lists the following truths about fear:

1. The fear will never go away as long as you continue to grow!
2. The only way to get rid of the fear of doing something is to go out and . . . do it!
3. The only way to feel better about yourself is to go out and . . . do it!
4. Not only are you afraid when facing the unknown, so is everyone else!
5. Pushing through fear is less frightening than living with the bigger underlying fear that comes from a feeling of helplessness!

What Can We Learn from This?

Feelings are always real. There's no point in denying the feeling itself, just as when someone tells you there's nothing to be afraid of. That advice has never helped anybody. The feeling (fear, worry, or whatever) is real. But that doesn't mean you have to let it govern your life. And there you have the key. Even though the fear is real, there are ways to check it so that it won't paralyze you.

If you accept that there will always be things to be afraid of, that you are always going to worry about certain moments in your life, you will find it easier to deal with these feelings when they pop up. To be even clearer: You can't protect yourself from negative feelings.

When I coach individual clients, I often find that they expect that life must feel perfect all the time. But that won't happen. It's completely impossible, and there's absolutely no point in aiming for it. Perfect happiness free from all negative feelings is a utopian state that is never going to be achieved.

It would be just as ridiculous to try to ignore negative feelings and hide from them. However hard it may seem, you have to realize that difficult feelings are part of life and you need to confront them head-on.

You need to learn to live with a degree of fear and a degree of worry. Guilty feelings arise when you haven't taken responsibility for yourself or for those you care about. But you don't need to feel guilt for trying to liberate yourself from somebody who exploits you. From now on, that person will have to take care of themselves.

So how do you learn to live with fear?

Answer: You do exactly what you're afraid of. The psychology here is extremely simple. It works in the same way as trying to cure someone of a phobia like fear of spiders. The person gradually exposes themselves to a harmless spider or two until they finally discover that spiders aren't actually dangerous (gross, maybe, but very rarely dangerous). That's an extremely brief description, and naturally the process is a bit more complex, but basically that's what it's all about. You need to expose yourself to what you're afraid of.

If you are afraid of the dark, a therapist will ask you to sit in the darkness for a short time until you realize that it isn't dangerous. The same applies to fears that develop after you've crashed your car or fallen off a horse. You get up in the saddle again, even if doing so feels scary.

If you're afraid of not giving in to your partner's demands, compare that fear with the feeling you get in your body when you—unwillingly—go along with that demand. Imagine that your partner has been pushing you for some kind of strange sex you dislike or that they want you to commit to something that raises alarm bells in your head. You can imagine whatever that would be for you. You know they're going to be angry/surly/grumpy, and they'll try lots of manipulation techniques when you refuse—all to get you to change your mind and go along with what they're demanding. But what does it feel like to agree to their weird demand? How do you feel when you do that? Do you feel powerless and used? Is dealing with their bad mood really worse than the way you will feel if you give in to them?

Feel the fear—and do it anyway. Say no, using the technique I described earlier. Remember what I said before: You deserve better.

You're always going to experience negative feelings in life. You can't fully protect yourself from them, but you can choose who is going to trigger them—you or somebody else. Take responsibility for yourself and your own life and spell it out, loud and clear, when you're being manipulated.

Think about this: Everybody feels worry and fear when they leave their comfort zone, but nevertheless there are people who ignore these feelings and "just do it," even though they're afraid. Fear isn't the problem. The problem is how you choose to handle it.

And remember this: Thoughts aren't dangerous. What do I mean by that? Fear and worry exist in your mind as thoughts and feelings. It's in your skull that you start worrying that your wife is going to be mad, that she'll give you the silent treatment the entire weekend, that she's going to cry and fuss because you haven't agreed to her unreasonable demands. That happens inside your head, and before it happens it's not real. You can change your thoughts as easy as pie.

A positive thought to counter this fear and worry could be this: *Now I have the tools I need to regain control of my own life.*

4. Put the Manipulation into Words

As long as the understood contract between you and the manipulator remains intact, the manipulation will also remain intact. You need to break that contract and clearly say what you're experiencing.

There is no point moping around the office or at home with a wounded expression: Nobody is going to be able to read your thoughts. What you need to do is confront the manipulator with your perspective on what is happening. This can be done in private, in a calm manner. You don't need to arrange an elaborate dinner and make a big thing of it, but do make sure that you can talk for a while without being disturbed.

Plan what you need to say. I'll give you a framework that you can adapt to your own situation. Be sure to include every step to avoid misunderstandings.

This is what you should say:

1. When you . . . *(describe what the manipulator is doing that you want them to stop doing)*
2. I feel . . . *(describe exactly what sort of negative feeling is created)*
3. If you stopped . . . *(the objectionable behavior)* and instead . . . *(describe what kind of behavior you want to see in this given situation)*
4. Then I am going to feel . . . *(describe exactly what feeling you want to have with your partner/boss/colleague/mother or whomever the manipulator is)*

You need to say exactly those things in exactly that order. That way your message will be understood and there's a good chance that the manipulator will actually listen to you. If they're essentially a reasonable person who has simply gotten stuck behaving in a harmful manner, then you'll see them change if you use this method.

Here's an example from a situation I coached someone through a few years ago:

1. *When you raise your voice and shout at me . . .*
2. *I feel afraid and worried.*
3. *If you stopped shouting and instead asked me in a calm voice . . .*
4. *then I would feel more respected and valued by you.*

Here is another example:

When you say that you're lonely all the time, I feel inadequate and unhappy. If, instead of going on about your loneliness,

*you would tell me what you did today, it would give me a feel-
ing of calm and security.*

At your workplace it might sound like this:

*When you call me an incompetent idiot, I feel totally worth-
less and just want to go home. If, instead of questioning my
intelligence, you would actually point out the mistakes I've
made and suggest what I ought to do differently, that would
help me develop my work and do a better job.*

If you are feeling strong on this particular day, you might even be
a bit bolder:

*When you always complain that you aren't feeling good and
imply that it's my fault, you make me experience paralyzing
guilt. If, instead of lazing in bed with imaginary illnesses,
you were to get up, get dressed, and do something useful for
once, then it would allow me to believe that this relationship
is worth saving.*

Now we've broken a pattern, haven't we? You are going to be surprised at the reaction you'll get.

As you can see, every single statement follows steps 1–4. It's not a
bad idea to get out a pencil and paper and start writing things down.
What situation and person do you think of first? How does that person's behavior make you feel? What would you like to see from now
on? And how would you like to feel instead? Use the formula, write
your statement, and read it out aloud to yourself a few times.

When you explain your attitude to the manipulator, do it in a calm
and confident voice. I know, that's easier said than done, but practic-
ing a few times will make it a lot easier.

A good way of closing the conversation and making sure your meaning is completely clear is to say something like this:

> *I know that it's your choice to shout/cry/blame me, but now you know that it makes me feel unhappy/afraid/worthless/ insecure.*

Why is this important? Partly because you've repeated something the manipulator hadn't expected to hear from you. Partly because you've said that you see their behavior as a deliberate choice. You've also said that your feelings are your responsibility. If you had said that their behavior causes your feelings, this risks leading to discussions, and that can end with your imagining that your feelings are wrong and so on.

Now it's up to the manipulator to show whether they're going to be sensible or not.

5. Destroy the Manipulation Once and for All

This step is something that you'll probably be forced to do for some weeks, or even some months. Remember that you are in the process of regaining control of yourself, your feelings, and in fact your life. And it's worth it. Believe me.

The manipulator—your husband, your live-in partner, your boss, your colleague, your children, your mother, or that dreadful friend that you might need to give up on—is not going to take all this change well. The answer you'll receive after your statement from step 4 is most likely not going to be, *Oh! I had no idea! Sorry, I'll stop that immediately.*

No, changing behavior takes time. Making the switch from bad behavior to good behavior can take months, which is why I want to remind you of the power of consistency.

Once you've put your cards on the table, that's it.

If you say that you won't accept a certain behavior, then you have to follow through. If your manipulator should happen to be a psychopath, they'll play along with your conditions right away and look for inconsistencies in your response. They'll then stick the knife in even deeper once they've found your weak spots.

Consistency is powerful.

When the manipulator falls back to their usual tricks—the silent treatment, shouting, cursing, slamming doors, slamming their fist on the table, angry looks, scornful laughter, tears, sulking, nasty comments, sighing, generally ignoring you, threatening you, or whatever it is that your particular manipulator has succeeded with before—then you firmly say, "I understand that you want me to do/not to do that, but your tactic won't work."

Some examples:

- I know that you want me to do the job for you, but your threats won't work on me any longer.
- I realize that you want me to go with you tomorrow, but ignoring me and subjecting me to the silent treatment is not going to have any effect.
- I can see that you want me to do that, but your anger and your swearing simply won't work any longer.

Calmly explain to them:

I know what you're doing and it won't work any longer. Drop it.

The manipulator is going to need to try something else. Or start behaving in a respectful manner toward you.

6. Explain Your Conditions for Your Continued Relationship

This is easier in a personal relationship than at your workplace. If you have a manipulative boss, that will affect your decision. One of the best pieces of advice I was given (by one of the best bosses I've ever had) was that you should choose your boss. With the wrong boss, you're not going to get anywhere. And unfortunately, you don't get to decide what you boss does. You can only appeal to their common sense and hope that they are smart enough to see the importance of what you're saying. If your boss really doesn't listen, perhaps it's time for you to think about a career somewhere else.

On the home front, it's a bit easier. You can say to your partner, to your mother, to your brothers and sisters that you're prepared to ditch them if they don't behave in a respectful manner.

I know—again, that is easier said than done. But if you've identified that you are living with a manipulator, then you also know why you feel bad. And if you've read this far, I'm guessing you'll want to know what to do now.

To avoid an unnecessary breakup, you can explain what your conditions are for a normal relationship. This is not the time to try and gain all the control for yourself. It's not about payback for the past. That would entail behaving exactly like the manipulator who has created the problem, and I know you are above that. But you do need to explain a couple of things before you're both ready to move on. You're going to establish a sort of rule book for certain parts of your relationship.

This is what I suggest you do:

1. Explain that from now on you are going to make your own decisions regarding what you are, or are not, willing to do in your relationship. In making those decisions, you are going to consider

your own needs as well as the needs of others (including the manipulator).

2. Explain to the manipulator how you want to be treated—for instance, that you want to be treated with respect, as a person who deserves honesty and consideration; that you want the manipulator to show that they value you as a partner (or daughter or lover or whatever). Say straight out that you will not allow yourself to be hurt in your relationship.

3. Establish a defined framework and limitations. Tell them that manipulation techniques (preferably naming those that you have observed) will not be tolerated. Do not use threats; they will only make the situation worse. Just explain that you aren't going to take part in any sort of dialogue that includes manipulation.

4. Ask the manipulator to confirm that you have needs, principles, opinions, and values that—even if they don't coincide with those of the manipulator—are not wrong. Explain that just because they think they are right does not mean that you are automatically wrong.

5. Explain that you expect a higher standard in your relationship from now on and that you have established clear limits for your personal integrity.

6. Finally, ask (perhaps with a friendly smile and gentle eyes) the manipulator to confirm that they've listened to and fully understood your message—and that they're going to make an effort in the future.

That's it.

Once again, it's not likely that the person who has manipulated you, perhaps for years, will simply say, "Sure, no problem." But if you've followed the earlier six steps in your plan to rebuild your personal integrity, this conversation will not come as a complete surprise.

When you are preparing to explain these things, new fears, worries, and some guilty feelings are going to appear. Be prepared for that. Resist the instinct to back down. Remember, it isn't the fear that is the problem—it's what you do with it. Why not go pick up a copy of *Feel the Fear—and Do It Anyway*? Now you have your chance to really transform a dysfunctional relationship.

In the best-case scenario, the manipulator will gradually adopt a new way of doing things. With the help of your decisiveness and, above all, your consistent behavior, perhaps this really will create a new dynamic in your relationship. This could very well be what brings you both to new heights.

A Dose of Realism

There is always a risk that the manipulator says that's the end of it and leaves you. That could happen, and it proves one thing: It wasn't about you. Not really. It was about what you could give the manipulator, and now they want that from somebody else. If they can't live in your relationship entirely on their own terms, they're not going to have anything to do with you.

And that is the answer to the question: Is this relationship really worth investing in?

17

What If Nothing Works?

Fact: A psychopath is born every 47 seconds.
—Kent A. Kiehl, *The Psychopath Whisperer:*
The Science of Those Without Conscience

Or how to protect yourself from a full-blood psychopath.

Remarkably, there are many people who live under the delusion that they can "cure" a psychopath. That is a fairly common explanation for why some people are attracted to imprisoned violent criminals. Around the world, criminals are locked up for murder, manslaughter, rape, assault, torture, pedophilia, and other horrific things. Nevertheless, these violent offenders receive more letters from people thirsting for love than all the other prisoners. Typically, the criminals are men and their adoring pen pals are women.

Why? (Apart from the obvious fact that some people are just disturbed.) It's not unlikely that these "fans" would even be willing to commit serious crimes themselves. Some studies show that, for example, violent women often stick together with violent men.

There's also the question of poor self-esteem. To be involved with a dangerous criminal can grant someone a certain status. What's more dangerous than someone who kills? There's also a sort of strange narcissism at play here. *Sure, he killed other women or raped them, but I'm different. I can fix him.* Dangerous.

The charm that many psychopaths possess is spellbinding. There are stories that you'd hardly believe if I told them. In little Sweden alone, murderers and violent criminals—who have been given long prison sentences for their horrible crimes—have started romantic relationships with their lawyers, with the *victim's* lawyers (!), with their psychiatrists, with psychologists who have diagnosed them as psychopaths, with police officers, and with prison staff. It isn't hard to work out why the psychopath sees value in such relationships, but the others? We're talking about people who should know better.

The worst example is when a psychopath even succeeds in fooling a specialist in psychiatry. Robert Hare, whom I have mentioned several times, also admits to having been fooled by a psychopath. If not even he could see the danger, what could happen to you and me?

But that's what it's like with psychopathy. It fascinates in a strange way; sometimes we even make the psychopath the hero. Take, for example, Dexter Morgan, the main character in the TV series *Dexter* that aired for eight seasons (a spoiler warning here if you haven't seen all the episodes). I've watched all eight seasons and thought they were good. Somewhere around season 4, I lost count of how many people he'd killed. If the average is one victim per episode, he must be one of the worst serial killers in the history of film, and if this had been real life . . . well. We'd be talking about hundreds of victims. (Don't send me emails about the exact body count; I admit I don't know, since I haven't counted.)

And nevertheless . . . we're fascinated by him.

But hang on a moment, you (if you've seen the series) are thinking. Dexter only murders murderers, so he actually does some good in society. Something like James Bond.

Umm. Taking the law into your own hands is never a good plan, and real-life violent psychopaths, unlike Dexter, can hardly control themselves. But regardless, he is forever putting his family at risk with his actions. At the beginning of the series, his wife is just a cover-up for his murderous activities. He wants to look normal. His wife gets her throat cut because of the things he's done. His own sister is murdered at the end of the series when she tries to protect him. He's remorseful, which makes him more human. The problem with his remorse is that in real life a psychopath with Dexter's murderous instincts wouldn't feel any sadness when people close to them suffer.

Be that as it may, we "support" Dexter in exactly the same way as some women support real-life psychopaths. They seek out psychopaths in prisons and listen to their stories about how they're actually the victims, wrongly convicted (they're innocent!) in a system that refuses to listen. Nobody understands them, and now at last comes a woman who gets them. They have plenty of sad stories about their terrible childhood. Of course, this has nothing to do with their psychopathy. With very few exceptions, psychopathy is something you are born with. It's not related to how your parents treated you.

There are some theories that you can create psychopathy by, for example, treating young people a certain way. In some African countries, nine-year-olds have been given cannabis and then a rifle, with which they were encouraged to shoot dead pigs. In a step-by-step process, this can create nine-year-olds who can mow down living people with AK-47s. But that isn't psychopathy. It's indoctrination and brainwashing, and a cruel way of blunting human empathy. The psychopath is the person who has gotten children to carry out the horrific deeds.

Many women think they can save a criminal, that they can cure the psychopath from their inner demons and make them "normal."

To claim that all the experts totally agree on whether this is possible would be an exaggeration (researchers never really agree with each other), but one thing is clear: It's not possible to cure psychopathy. It's a personality disorder caused by an abnormality in the brain. There is a lot of neurobiological research on the subject, and new findings are published every year. With the help of MRI scans, it's possible to determine exactly where in the brain the deviation is located: This is a slight simplification, but the amygdala (which helps process emotions and memories) seems to be involved. But as of now there is no way to cure psychopathy.

Medication doesn't work.

It's not possible to operate. And what would you operate on, anyway? Lobotomy has been considered unethical for decades.

All attempts to treat psychopathy therapeutically have failed. Therapy even seems to make things worse. Therapy is often about trying to understand your own actions, which is usually good. But if you explain to a psychopath how others suffer from their behavior, they'll only get new ideas. The literature on psychopathy contains numerous examples of psychopaths who used everything they have learned during therapy to go back into society and cause even more damage. After all, they've just been given an instruction book. Now they fake being normal even more realistically, which causes even more confusion. There only seems to be one thing that has an effect on a psychopath: age. Psychopaths tend to calm down slightly over the years.

I've come across a potentially psychopathic person on the edge of my circle of acquaintances. This man is not a violent person but uses more subtle methods. But there's no doubt that he has many psychopathic traits. We have mutual acquaintances, and when he's dissatisfied with the mutual acquaintance (his ex-wife), he'll send me an email and say that I ought to do something about her behavior. The weird thing is that he often references the fact that I specialize in behavior, which is presumably a way to tell me that I ought to understand the situation and see his ex-wife as the villain that he says she is.

On the surface, he's pleasant, social, extroverted, and charming. A bit of a one-track mind—and, to be honest, rather self-centered—but on the whole fairly harmless. A nice guy. If you don't live with him, you'd never believe that there was anything odd about him. He's surrounded by a large number of "pawns" in his private life as well as at work.

But there are some facts that present another picture. All his life, he has mirrored whomever he's living with at the time. The woman he was last married to, my acquaintance, was interested in gardening and home decoration. Her husband immediately became interested in digging holes all over the lawn. He stripped wallpaper and started renovating. The woman was always physically active, and when she started working out more seriously at the gym, he took on that interest as well. He trained several times a week and got into really good shape. He even appointed himself her personal trainer (grandiosity again), even though this was actually her specialty, not his.

None of this might seem especially strange. A lot of couples share experiences and hobbies and inspire each other. But there was a weird pattern in all this. When the woman bought a horse—an old dream of hers—and started taking riding lessons, the man also started riding. It got to the point that he was taking so many lessons that she couldn't take any. So while he practiced her interests, she had to stay at home looking after the kids. Soon, he had taken over her life and put her in the back seat.

When it comes to deviant behavior, we have to look at the patterns. Every one of us sometimes does things we can't explain, even to ourselves. The decisions we make aren't always logical. But when a certain behavior is repeated time after time, we should be cautious. Because it doesn't end there. The weird thing is that the man did the same thing to a woman with whom he had a previous relationship. That woman was an elite gymnast, and that became his primary interest, too. He didn't go to the gym, garden, or ride horses then. And in the relationship he's living in now, he no longer does any of those things. Nowadays, he arranges weddings, because that's what the latest woman does. She works as a wedding planner, and so he isn't interested in gardening, home decoration, horses, bodybuilding, or gymnastics.

But as a behavior expert, I ought to know better and support him in his . . . I don't know what. I've never understood what he wants from me.

I really didn't want to be involved in their conflict. I answered that my background in behavior allowed me to connect the dots, and that was why I ignored him. But, of course, he didn't stop. Finally, I gave him some hints about why his children refused to interact with him.

His reactions to my answers were interesting. He gave himself time to think it over; then, in some respects, started to behave "normally." He started talking as if he really cared, saying that he would take responsibility for his children. He even started pretending he had always behaved this way—as if the newly gained insight about parenting was something he'd always known. Many people around him believe it when he says that his kids mean everything to him. They hear what he says, but they're unaware of what he does for his children: absolutely nothing.

Now I don't answer his emails. I haven't given him any more advice; I just let him guess how he ought to behave. I honestly don't know how things turned out.

How to Handle a Real Psychopath

All specialists advise that you need to distance yourself from the psychopath. Forget about talking them out of the behavior, or getting them to understand that their conduct harms you or those close to you. Don't try to negotiate with the psychopath or believe that you can have a healthy level of contact. Any such contact would be on the psychopath's terms. They'll actively start to turn everyone in your life against you. They'll manipulate everyone they meet into believing that you're the villain.

You have to understand this isn't a typical psychiatric case and that the person is not going to change their behavior after medication or therapy. *They are never going to change.*

If you read the previous chapter and have followed my advice on how to take back control of yourself and your life, you'll know fairly soon whether the person you're dealing with is a psychopath or not. If your relationship has started to get back on track and this trend continues for several months, then you can count yourself lucky. If, however, you find yourself back in the same old pattern again, unfortunately there's only one solution: *Get up and go.*

That's the only thing that works. Create as much distance as possible between you and the psychopath. I know that this is a great deal easier to say than it is to do in real life. But it's the only thing you can do. You're simply a resource, a replaceable resource, for the psychopath.

I have acquaintances who have had to distance themselves from their parents because they are exhausting energy parasites. That was a hard decision, but you can't stay in an environment that hurts you.

Years ago, I left a relationship where I'd followed all the steps in the previous chapter. I made it clear that things must change if the relationship was going to survive.

The person in question didn't want to see my side of the issue, so I left. The way she sought to punish me tells me everything I need to know about how she valued me and our relationship. She demanded all the money I had, sued me for control of my company, and accused me of theft, insurance fraud, and a whole lot of other stuff. But she "loved" me . . . I recovered from that blow, but I know that the relationship was a hopeless case. A painful lesson, but now I have control over my life.

So my advice is this: *Get up and go.*

Don't try to fight the psychopath. Forget about retaliating. It isn't going to work. Don't expose them on social media and don't paint them as the psychopath they are. They're prepared for that and can counterattack. They will become even fiercer and will try to crush you without mercy if they think you are attacking them. And there is a high chance that they'll succeed. They've already spread their charming faux persona throughout their life. Their pawns are everywhere. While you were at work and supporting the family, they were phoning all sorts of people and communicating their version of you and your relationship. You're always going to be one step behind their conniving.

Yes, BUT, you might be thinking, *I can't just let them walk all over me!*

Exactly.

Get up and go.

You have to make a decision. You can't win this game, because you're human. You have feelings, you have an empathetic ability, and you feel remorse if you do harm to somebody. The psychopath doesn't feel any of this. For them, you are no more important than a beetle on the sidewalk. You're nothing. You mean nothing. You're just somebody who is in their way.

If you've fallen in love with a psychopath, if you happen to be married to a psychopath, if you discover that you have children with a psychopath, things will be extremely complicated.

Nevertheless . . .

Get up and go.

If you've just discovered that a colleague at work or your boss is a psychopath, then get a different job. Unless you can work under the radar, but what sort of work life would that be? Besides, you have no way of knowing what the psychopath might think up. Perhaps you'll be their next victim simply because they think it would be fun to see whether they can break you. You might stand in the way of their promotion. You must be gotten rid of. And they're going to get rid of you.

Get up and go.

Postscript: Some Words to Help You on Your Way

The trust of the innocent is the liar's most useful tool.

—Stephen King

My dear reader, I'm happy you've made it all the way to the end. If you've read *Surrounded by Idiots*, then you know that this book is a bit darker and perhaps not as lightly entertaining. But it was important for me to write this book when I noticed that some people were abusing the information in my first book for their own ends. Being Red is never an excuse for yelling at someone; blaming the fact that you're Yellow and don't like keeping your paperwork in order is not a justification for sloppiness. We all have the responsibility to behave respectfully and kindly toward each other and do our work well— regardless of our color.

To exploit people based on their colors is never acceptable. And now that you've read this book, you know what to do if that should ever happen to you. There are many examples of people who have fallen into the clutches of psychopaths, in their personal lives and at their workplace, and who have suffered from PTSD. Make sure this doesn't happen to you. And if it does happen to you, don't be afraid to seek professional help. CBT (cognitive behavioral therapy) has been shown to be extremely helpful in many cases. The most important thing is that you don't try to get through the possible trauma entirely on your own. Get help.

If you don't want to seek professional help, then at least read a book on the topic. At the end of this book, I've included some resources on psychopathy (for those of you who want to learn more about it) and on how you can further equip yourself to resist manipulation.

To those who want to know more about the colors and who haven't read *Surrounded by Idiots,* why not get ahold of a copy? It's available anywhere books are sold, as well as at public libraries. Why not take the opportunity to learn a great deal about the DISC profiles? It will save you a lot of time and headaches, at your workplace and in your personal life.

Should you go around worrying about meeting a psychopath? Is there reason to suspect everyone you meet from now on?

Of course not.

But knowledge is power.

Now you're aware that there are dangers you might not have considered before. You know that quite a lot of people have agendas and are prepared to do almost anything to achieve their own ends.

Let's be realistic: There are risks just driving a car. But that doesn't stop you from driving, does it? Think about it. When you sit behind the steering wheel in your car, you keep your eyes on the road and keep track of all the other drivers. This doesn't mean that everyone else on the highway is trying to crash into you. It just shows that you have a sensible approach to manage the risks involved in driving. If you keep track of everything around you, you'll be fine. You pay attention to traffic lights, you listen for emergency vehicles, you see the cyclist next to your car and give them enough room.

Just as you regularly look in the rearview mirror when you are driving, I want you to be vigilant when it comes to people you don't know or people that you know all too well by now. Consider how they behave and how they treat your relationship.

Remind yourself of what you've learned in this book. If a person has earned your trust, make sure they haven't earned it for life. What this (undoubtedly very lovely) individual did three months ago isn't worth anything if they suddenly start to treat you badly today. Always evaluate people by their current behavior, not their earliest.

The person you have in front of you is not the person they were a year ago; they're the person they were last night. Their real self is what they're showing now, not the fake personality they used when they snared you. That's the personality they wanted you to see. Remember that trust must be earned all the time.

Imagine a man who physically abuses his wife every day. Would you advise her to think of the children, the mortgage, her reputation, and how nice he was three years ago—and then encourage her to remain in the relationship?

No, of course you wouldn't. You would do whatever you could to help her get away from him.

And that's exactly what it's like to be the victim of a psychopath, a person with psychopathic traits, or an ordinary manipulator. This is about mental abuse, in some cases mental torture. It's not an option to stay, regardless of what other people are going to think, regardless of whether the children will now come from a "broken home," regardless of whether finances will be hard.

Abuse is abuse, regardless of whether it is physical or mental.

And, finally, you need to answer the question, *How much do you value yourself?*

Only you can answer that.

> Some lies are easier to believe than the truth.
> Brian Herbert and Kevin J. Anderson, *Dune*

Resources

Bentley, Barbara. *A Dance with the Devil: A True Story of Marriage to a Psychopath*. Berkley Publishing Group, 2008.

Black, Will. *Psychopathic Cultures and Toxic Empires*. Frontline Noir, 2015.

Boddy, Clive R. *Corporate Psychopaths*. Palgrave Macmillan, 2011.

Cascadia, Janet. *Tyranny of Psychopaths*. Self-published, CreateSpace, 2015.

Clarke, John. *Working with Monsters*. Random House Australia, 2002.

Cullberg, Marta. *In Depth Self-esteem: A Therapy to Repair Negative Self-Images*. Natur and Kultur, 2009.

Duvringe, Lisbet, and Mike Florette. *Female Psychopaths*, Ekerlid, 2016

Erikson, Thomas. *Surrounded by Idiots: How to Understand Those Who Cannot Be Understood*. Hoi forlag, 2014.

Evans, Patricia. *Controlling People*. Adams Media Corporation, 2002.

Forward, Susan, and Donna Frazier. *Emotional Blackmail*. William Morrow, 1998.

Gregory, Deborah W. *Unmasking Financial Psychopaths*. Palgrave Macmillan, 2014.

Hare, Robert D. *The World of a Psychopath*. Studentlitteratur, 2005.

Hintjens, Pieter. *The Psychopath Code*. Self-published, CreateSpace, 2015.

Hyatt, Christopher S., and Nicholas Tharcher. *The Psychopath's Bible*. Original Falcon Press, 2008.

Jeffers, Susan. *Feel the Fear and Beyond*. Vermilion, 2012.

————. *Feel the Fear—and Do It Anyway*. Vermilion, 2007.

Kiehl, Kent A. *The Psychopath Whisperer*. Oneworld Publications, 2015.

Lindwall, Magnus. *Self-Esteem Beyond Popular Psychology*. Studentlitteratur, 2011.

Lingh, Sigvard. *Everyday Psychopaths*. Recito, 2011.

McKenzie, Jackson. *Psychopath Free*. Berkley Publishing Corporation, 2015.

McNab, Andy, and Kevin Dutton. *The Good Psychopath's Guide to Success*. Corgi, 2015.

Naslund, Gorel Kristina. *Get to Know the Psychopath*. Natur and Kultur, 2004.

Ronson, Jon. *The Psychopath Test*. Picador, 2012.

Shelby, Richard. *Hunting a Psychopath*. Booklocker.com, 2015.

Tornblom, Mia. *More Self-esteem*. Forum, 2006.

————. *Self-esteem Now!* Forum, 2005.

Index

HIGH D/RED	HIGH I/YELLOW	HIGH S/GREEN	HIGH C/BLUE
Dominant	Inspiring	Stable	Analytical
Proactive	Extroverted	Patient	Investigative
Ambitious	Persuasive	Reliable	Cautious
Strong-willed	Verbal	Attentive	Systematic
Problem solver	Open	Restrained	Precise
Energetic	Positive	Lovable	Logical
Competitive	Empathetic	Persevering	Conventional
Forceful	Optimistic	Good listener	Distant
Inquisitive	Creative	Friendly	Objective
Direct	Spontaneous	Cautious	Perfectionist
	Sensitive	Supportive	

(page 95)

(page 54)

THE BASIC PILLARS IN DISC

Task-oriented
and issue-oriented

COMPLIANCE		DOMINANCE

How you react to rules and regulations	How you approach problems and deal with challenges

Waiting / Introvert — Action / Extrovert

How you react to change	How you cooperate with and try to influence other people

STABILITY		INFLUENCE

Person and
relationship-oriented